MINDWORKS

a spiritual journey

Volume 4

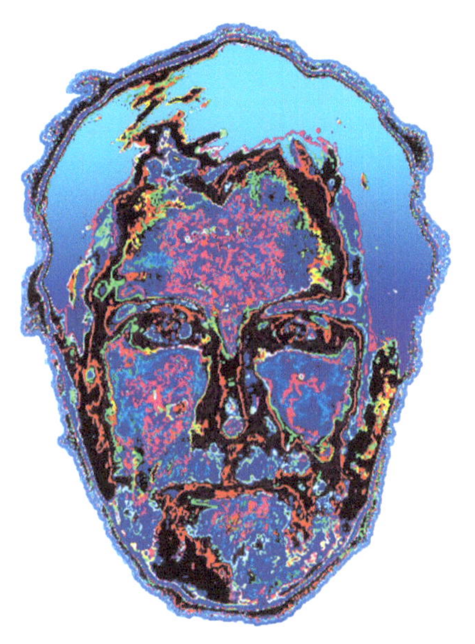

by Richard Fisher

Website: http://www.MINDWORKSart.com
Email: richard@mindworksart.com

ISBN 978-0-9852985-4-8

Printed by www.lulu.com

Front Cover: *Oz Head*

The origin of this image is a photo of my head which was modified with filters in Photoshop program. The Wizard of Oz is a 'humbug', an ego--not a god who originates images but the one who channels these images into the world.

Back Cover: *Life Is Difficult, Detail*

Dr.KENNETH RING, President of International Association for Near-Death Studies: IANDS.com believes that "...death itself, (is) really nothing more than the shifting of a person's consciousness from one level of the hologram of reality to another."
~MICHAEL TALBOT,
The Holographic Universe, 1991

Introduction

One's ego-mask, the persona, was not apparent to me for many years. It is only recently that I have become more aware of it and the role it plays in our lives. It is also clear now that since the beginning of my artistic life, a higher-self has played an important, albeit an unconscious role...that in fact I have always been a channel for these images, these designs and artworks that have come through me. Of course it seemed that "I did it"...that I created all these images, but of course it is not true and it is liberating to know that I am "the way"...the channel for this work.

During my life I have explored many venues of artistic possibilities; the common thread has always been visual arts, graphic and decorative design for printing on the surfaces of various products, always outward-oriented, the marketplace. Inward focus became possible with fine arts, studying oil painting at the Brooklyn Museum Art School with Reuben Tam, and later printmaking at Columbia University, Teachers' College.

A wonderful tool for turning inward is the work of Betty Edwards, *Drawing on the Right Side of the Brain* and *Drawing on the Artist Within.* There were other influences as well: Carl Jung, Leonardo da Vinci, Odion Redon and the teachings of Eckhart Tolle, *The Power of Now.* As Tolle says, "When your consciousness is directed outward, mind and world arise. When it is directed inward it realizes it's own Source and returns home into the Unmanifested." The challenge is to become more conscious in our work as well as in our lives.

The images in this book are mostly from the years 2010-2012. Craftsmanship and technique have always interested and challenged me, digital imagery being the latest. It is an adventure of discovery, of failures and successes,
the visual world of art opening up every step of the way.
What better way to realize one's self than being an artist.

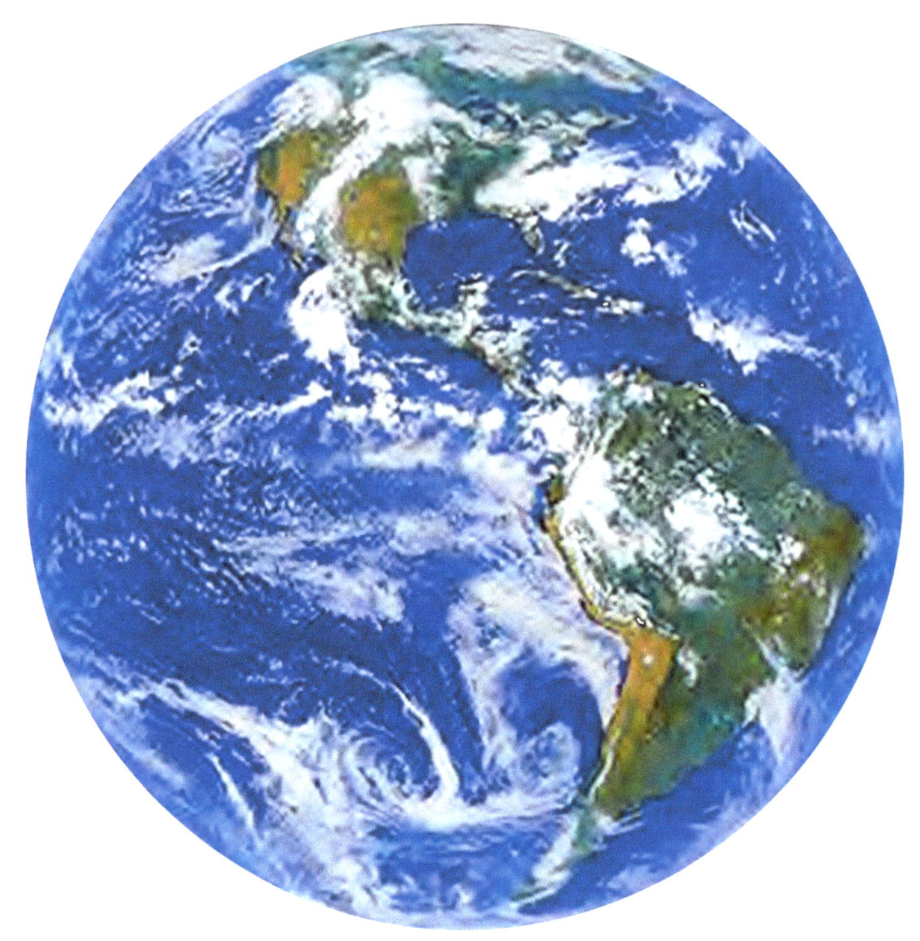

GAIA

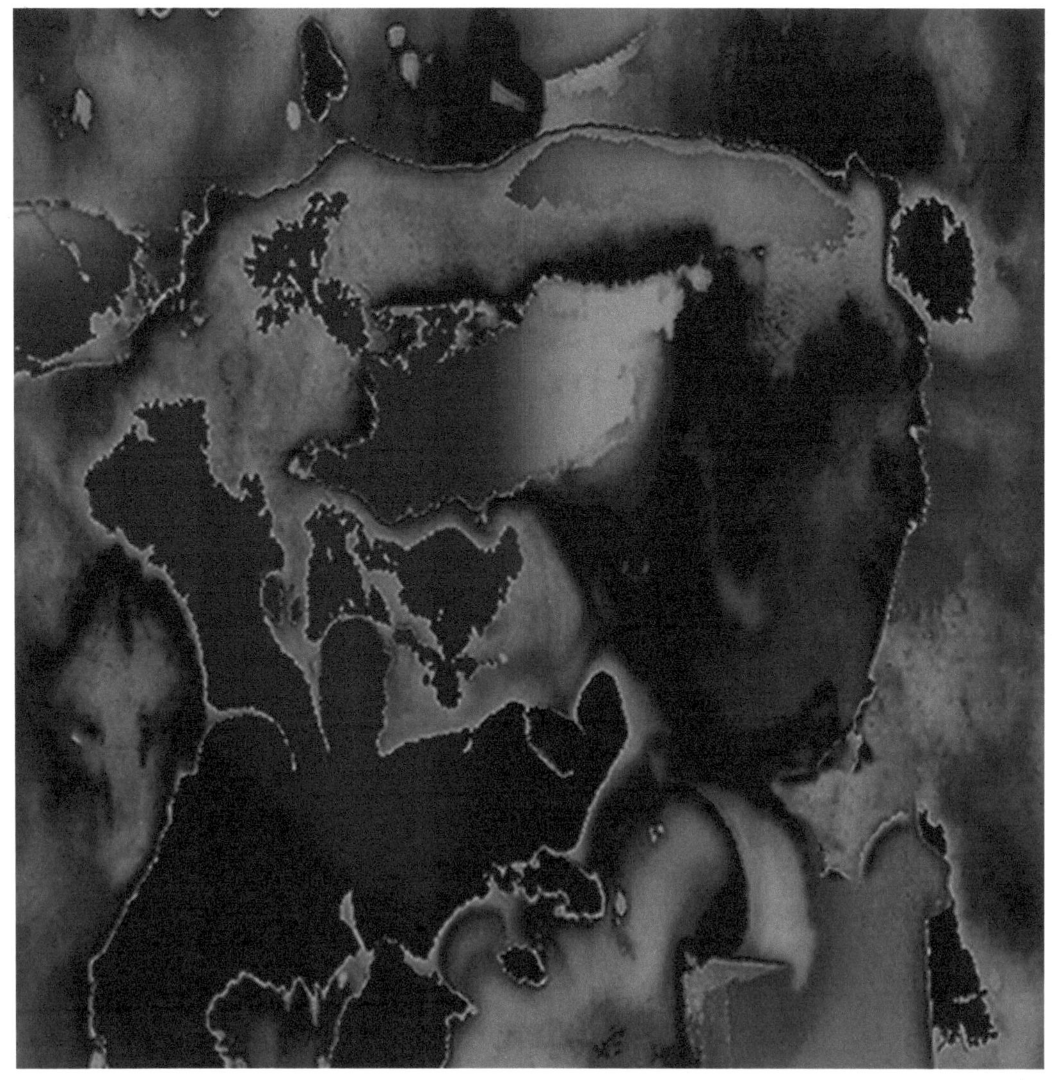

DoppelGanger, Artist

"At present, neurology doesn't know how memory works, or how brain cells turn raw data into complex thought, or where identity is located. If we knew these things, there might be no need to speculate about 'extended mind, extended consciousness,' the notion that thinking can occur outside the brain."
~DEEPAK CHOPRA, Life After Death, 2006

Angel On High

"I asked the light...
What is the Plan?
There is no plan...
there never was.
You are given this
universe to do what
you want and
you're free to do that."
~Mellen-Thomas,
Messages from the Light

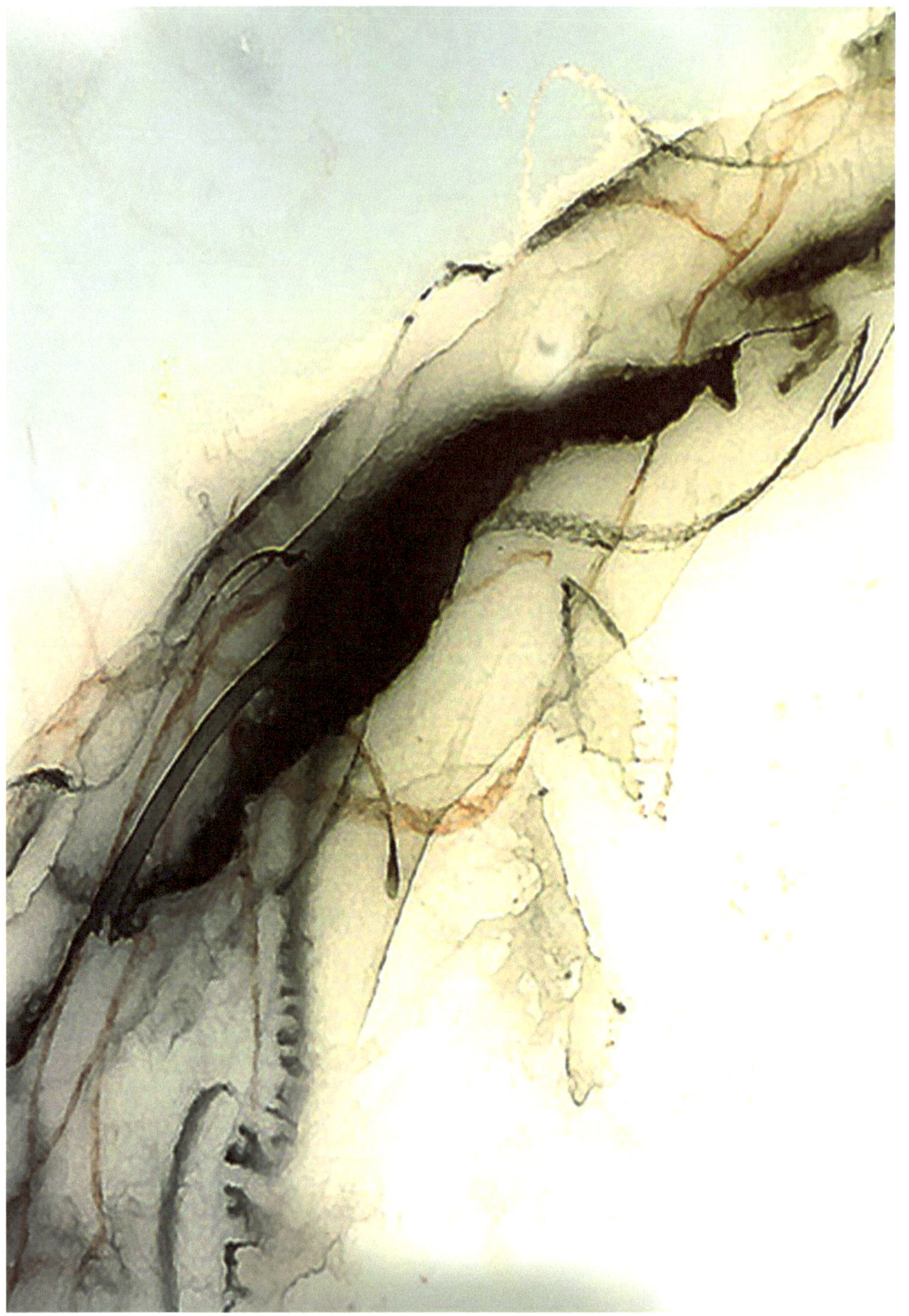

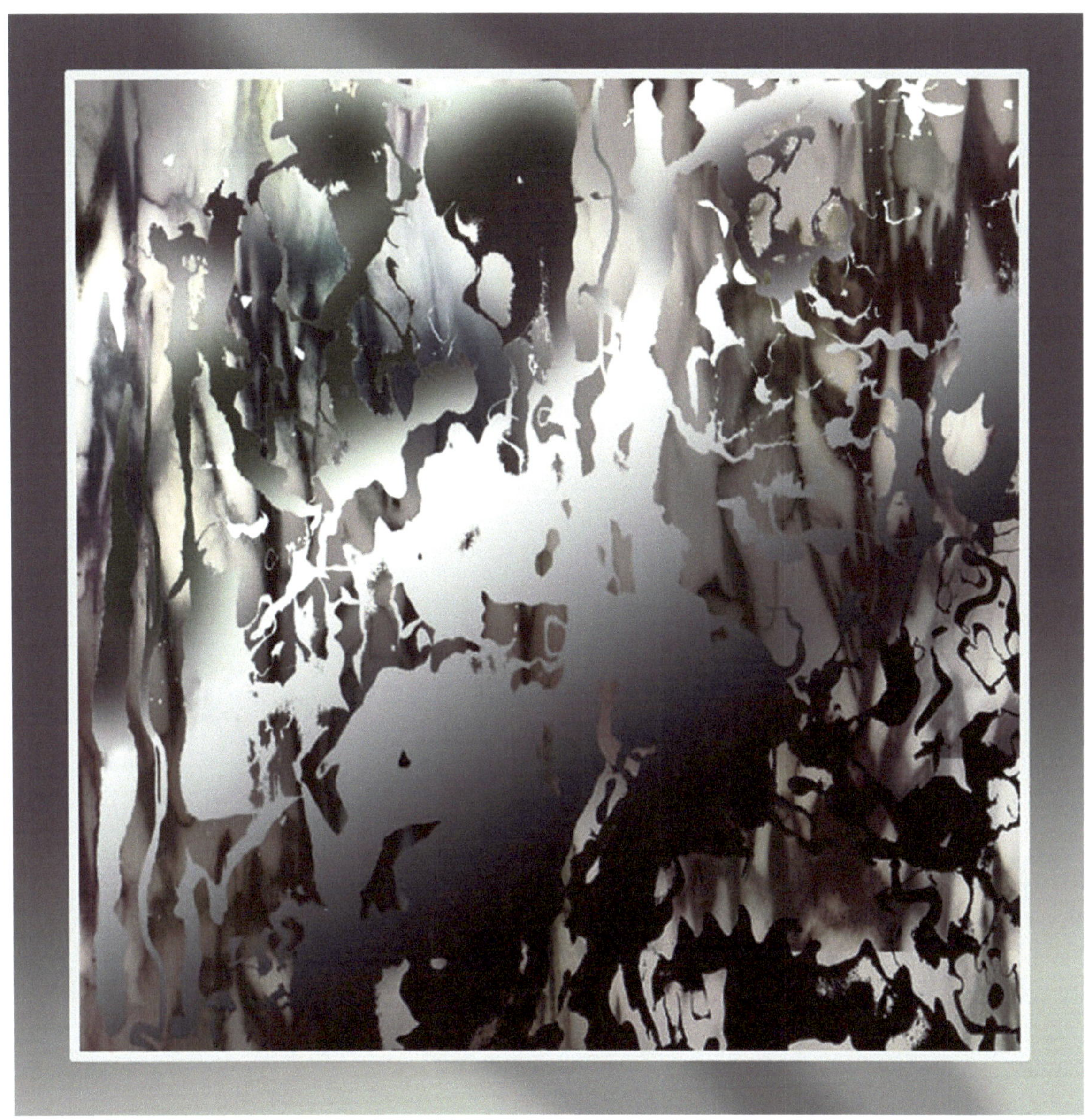

Conscious Effort,
Detail 6

"Become not only aware of your mental activity, but also of the consciousness that is witnessing your mind field."
http://www.yoga-mind-control.com

Quantum Leap

"By watching the mechanics of the mind,
you step out of its Resistance Patterns,
and you can then allow the present moment to be."

~ECKHART TOLLE,
The Power of NOW, 2001

"When asked whether one must seek for one's soul ..."No, don't worry, it will find you. My higher self is seeking me. My 'one mind' seeks to find my many scattered minds."

~Carlo Suares... teacher of the Cabala
~FRED ALAN WOLF, Taking the Quantum Leap,1981/'89

It is possible to rotate this image, to view it from 4 sides, to enhance your mediative experience

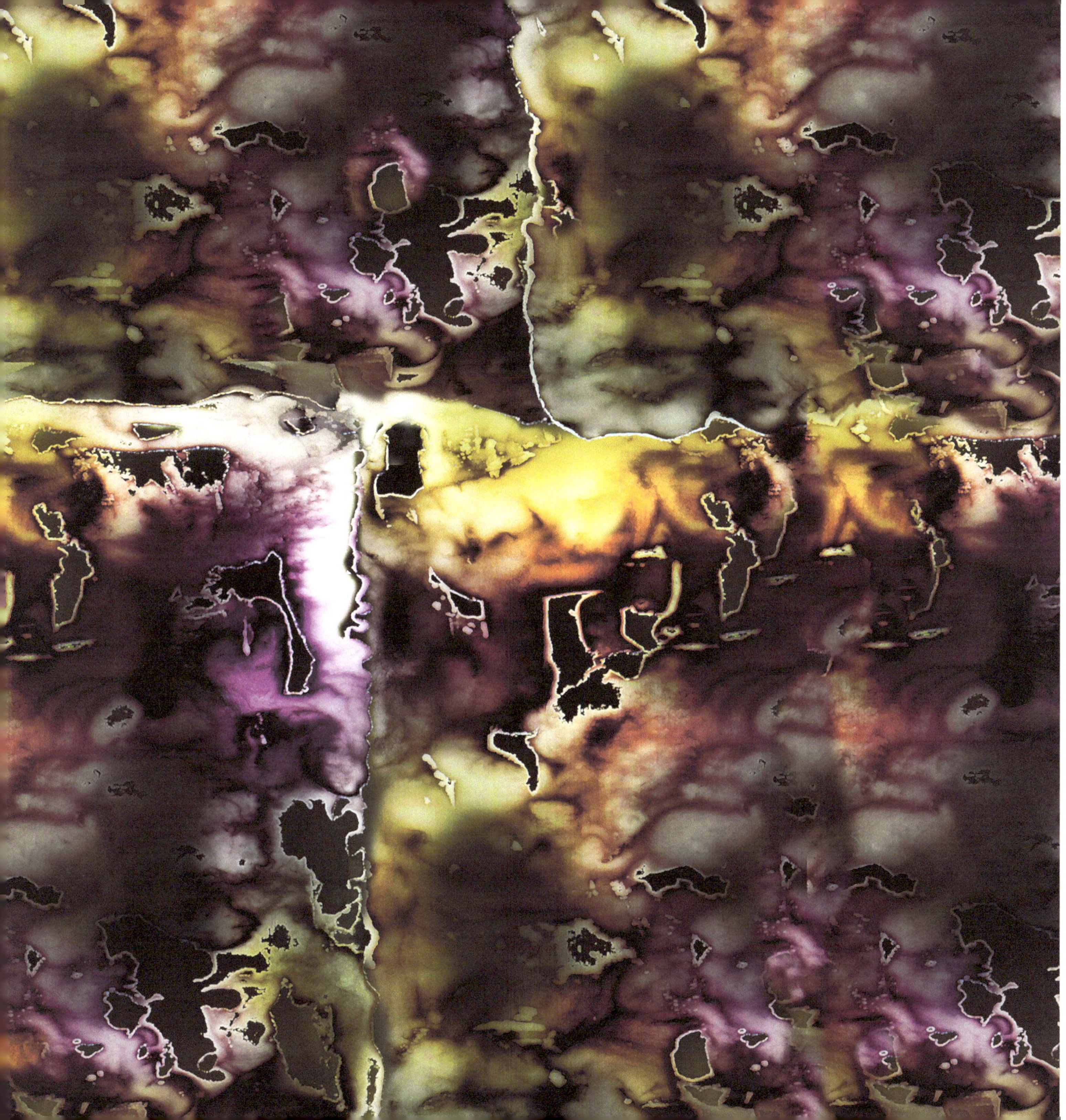

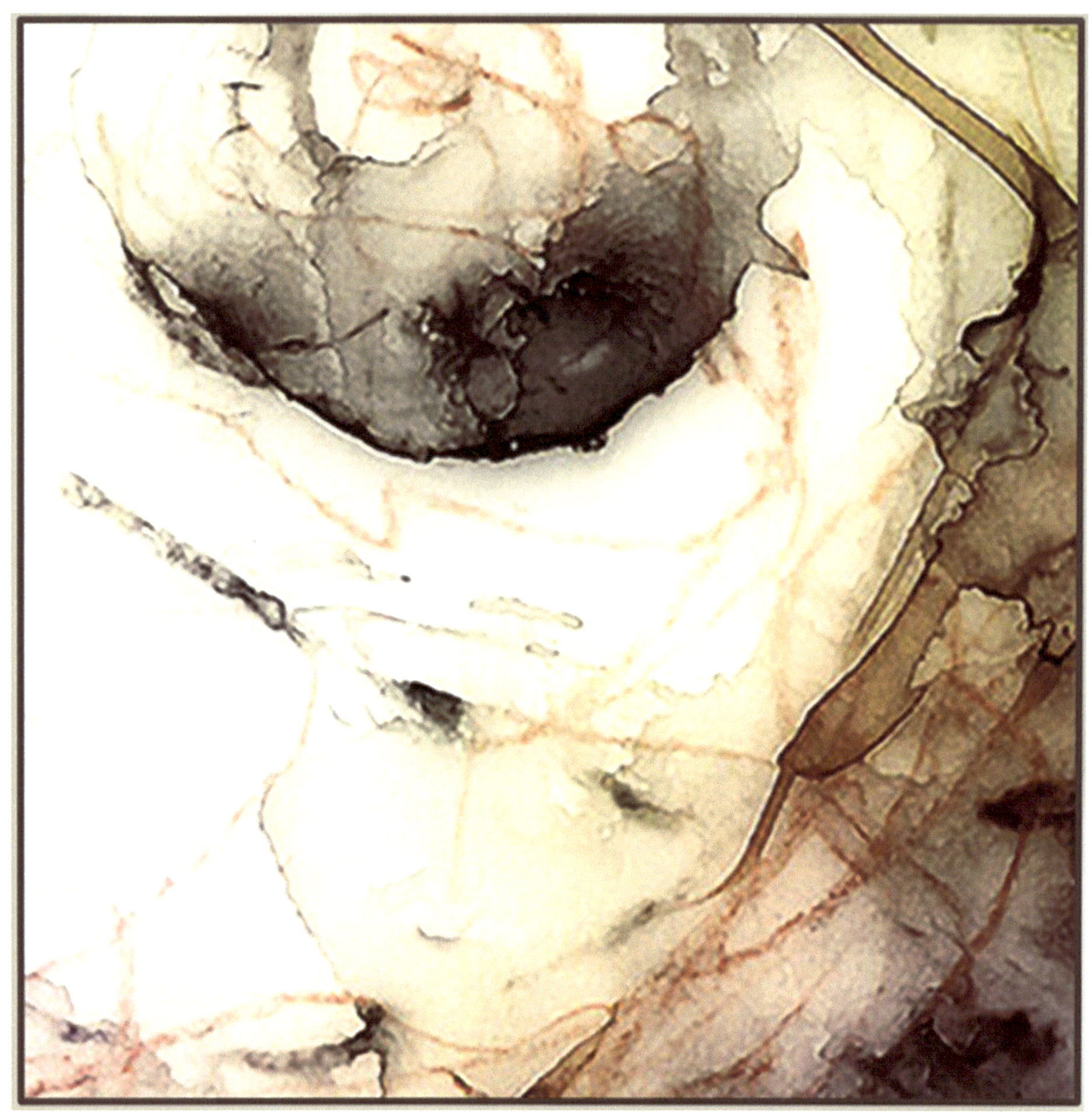

Child of GAIA

"We are made of light at our core. We come from the light, we're made of light, we return to the light, it's all about light."
~Mellen-Thomas, Messages from the Light

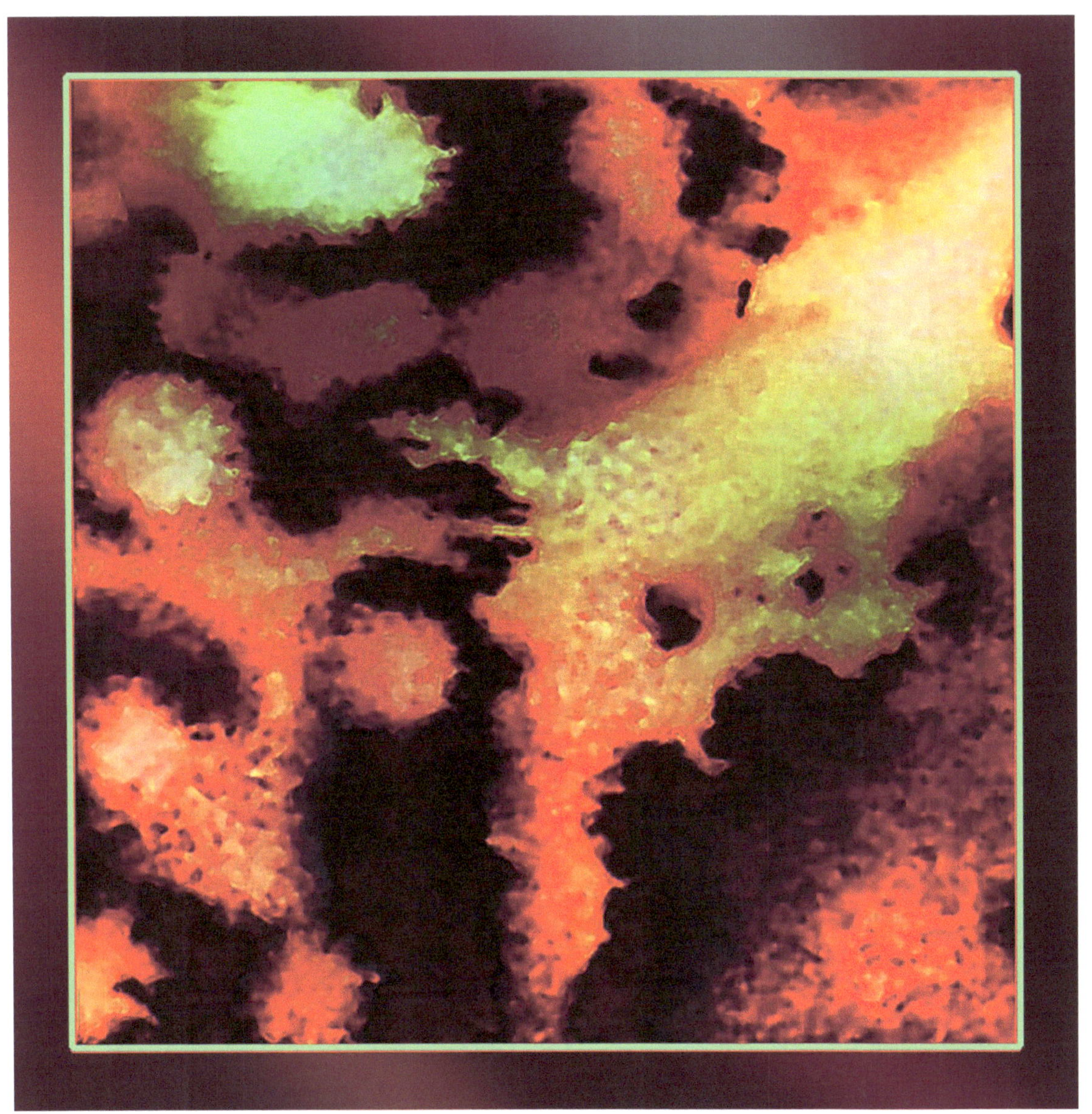

Lynn's Bright Night

"The quantum wave of probability (the qwiff) is still spreading out in space waiting for some unsuspecting observer to 'pop' it ...altering the probability and suddenly creating an observed reality."

~FRED ALAN WOLF, Taking the Quantum Leap, 1981

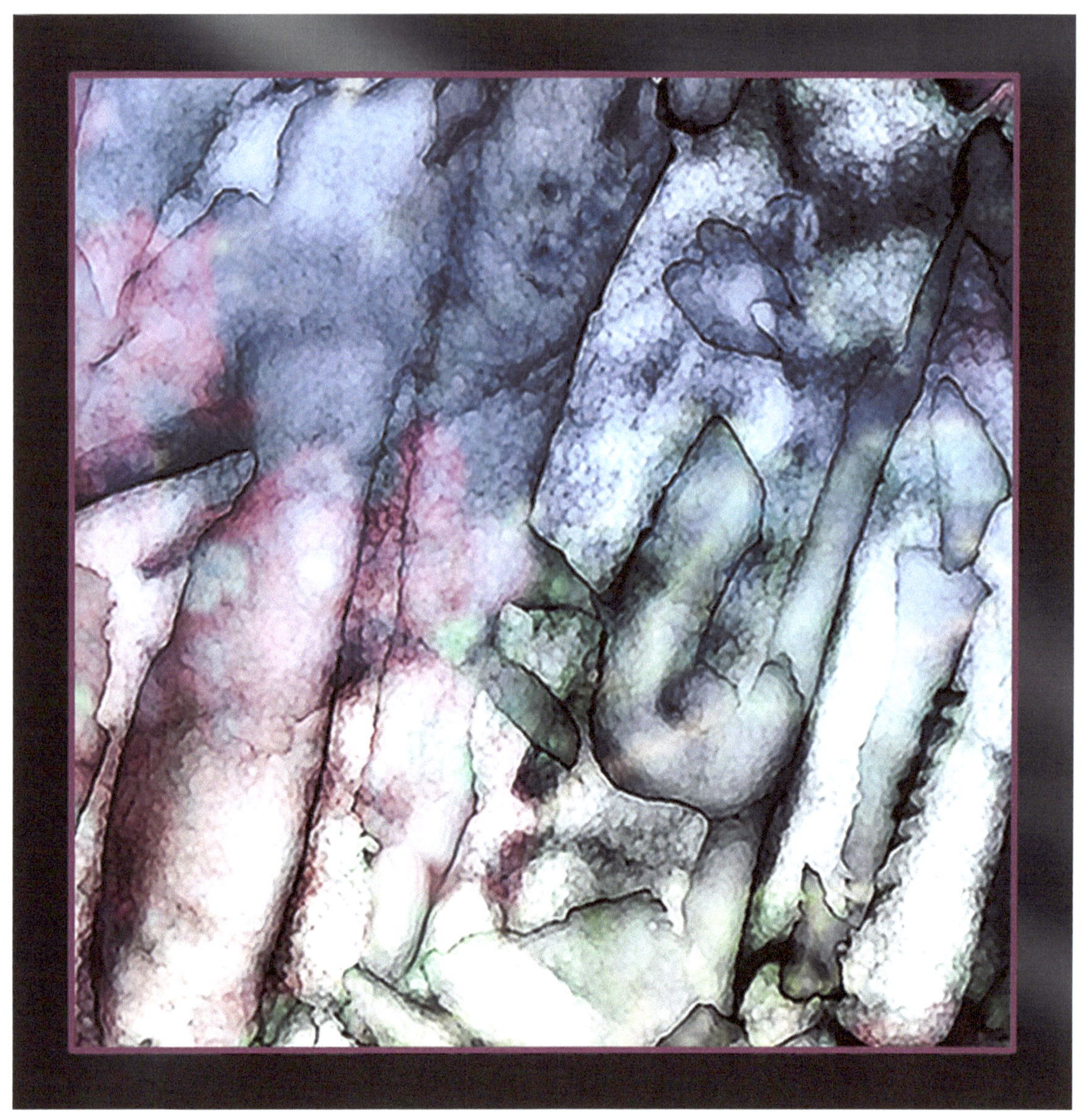

A Positive Reason

"In the Indian tradition, we are reborn, after all, for a positive reason, to express and exhaust the force of desire."
~DEEPAK CHOPRA, Life After Death, 2006

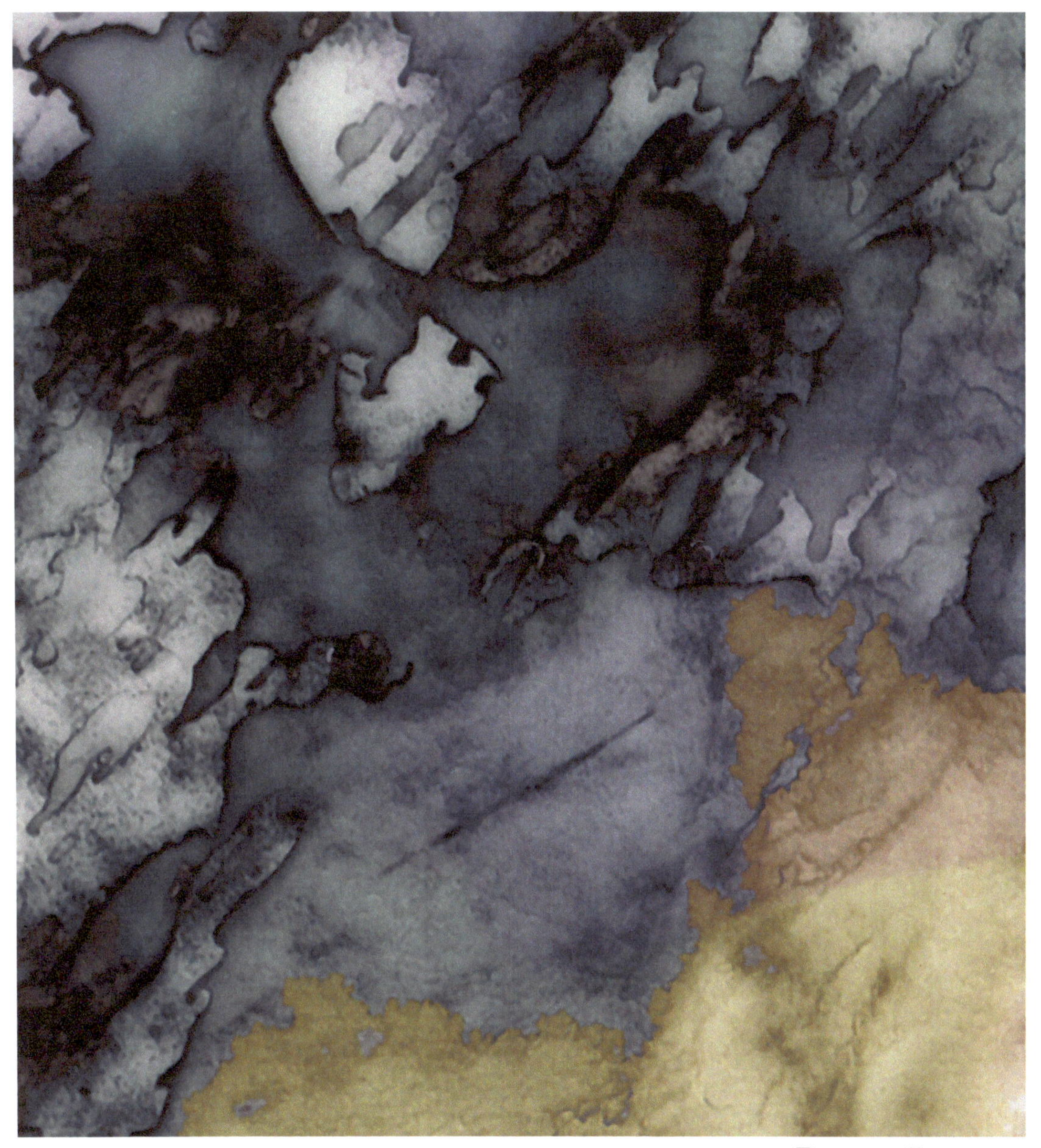

Being Longing

"In the very act of observation, the objective, 'real' world
appears and the subjective observer vanishes.
We know not how to observe ourselves."

~FRED ALAN WOLF, Taking the Quantum Leap 1981/1989

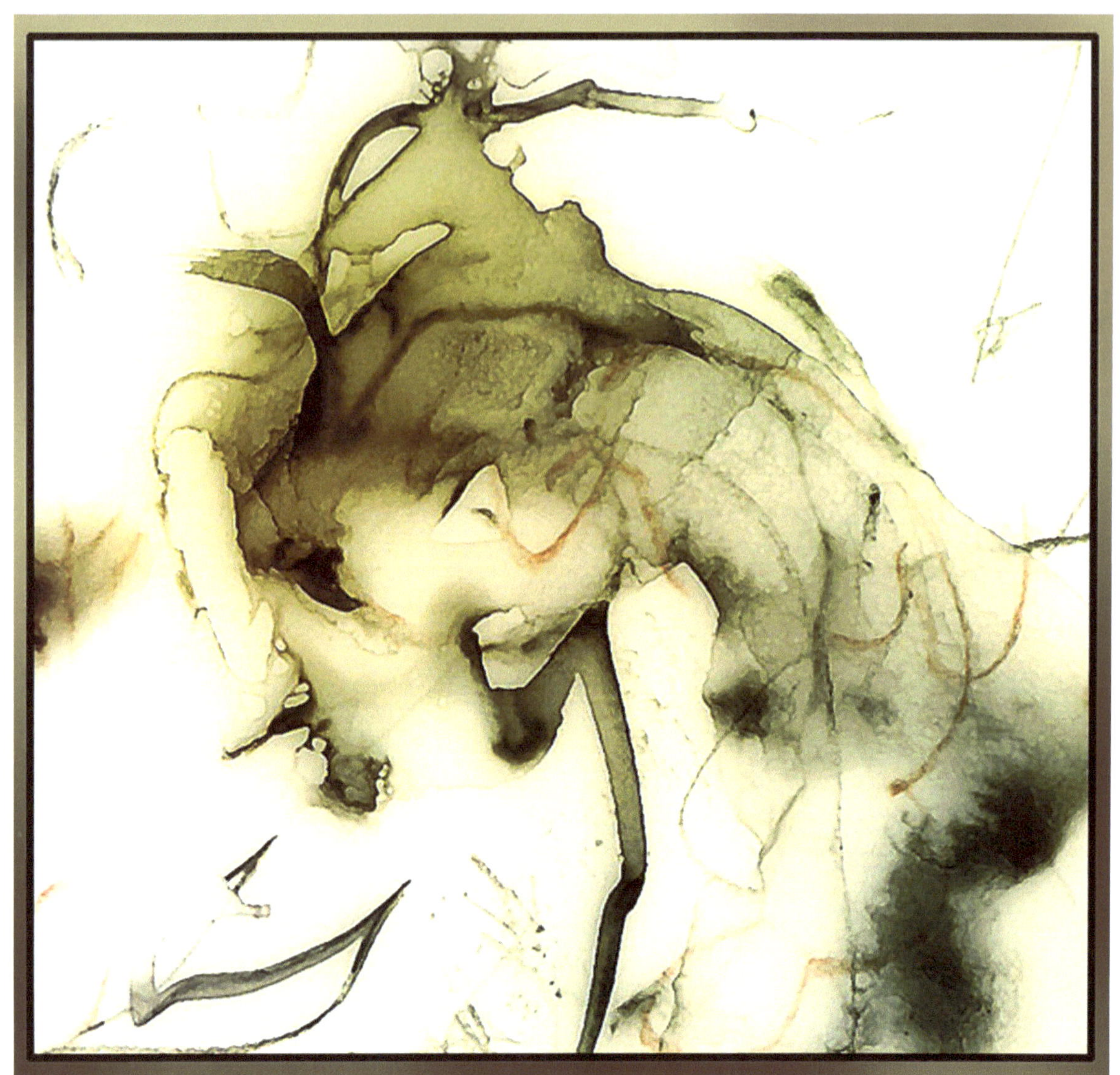

Colt

"Because creativity demands patience, skill, expectation, desire and openness, it leads us to another place where we learn to see in the dark. Nothing is said directly in a creative work; it is obliquely suggested."
~JOHN O'DONOHUE, Beauty, 2004

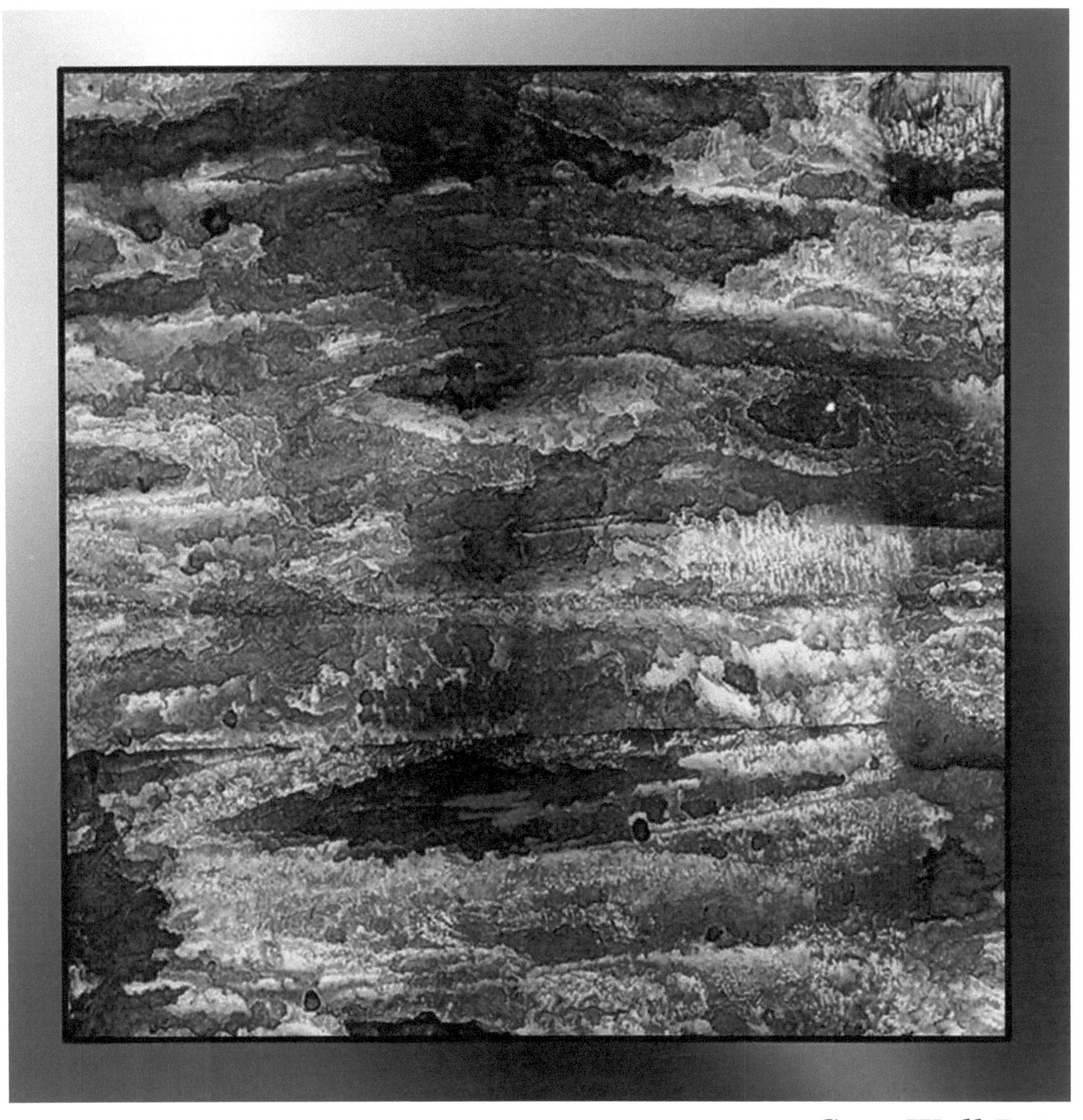

Cave Wall Being

"Look humanity.
Look at what you can do.
See who you are."
~PAT RODERGAST, Emmanuel's Book, 1985

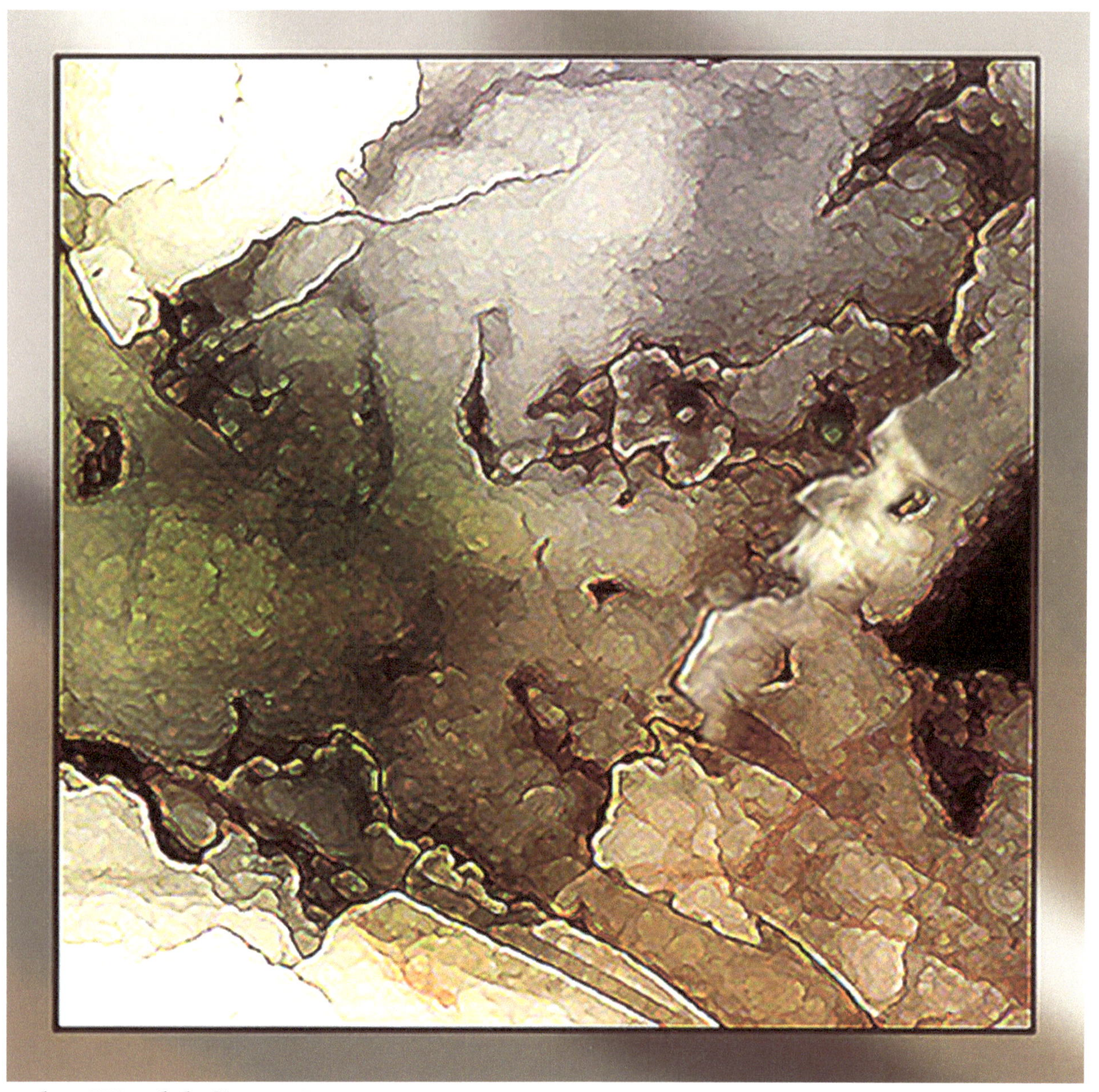

As the World Goes By

"Nuclear biology, Quantum Biology--looking at the nuclear state, your atoms as biology--first and foremost we are made of atoms."
~Mellen-Thomas, Messages from the Light

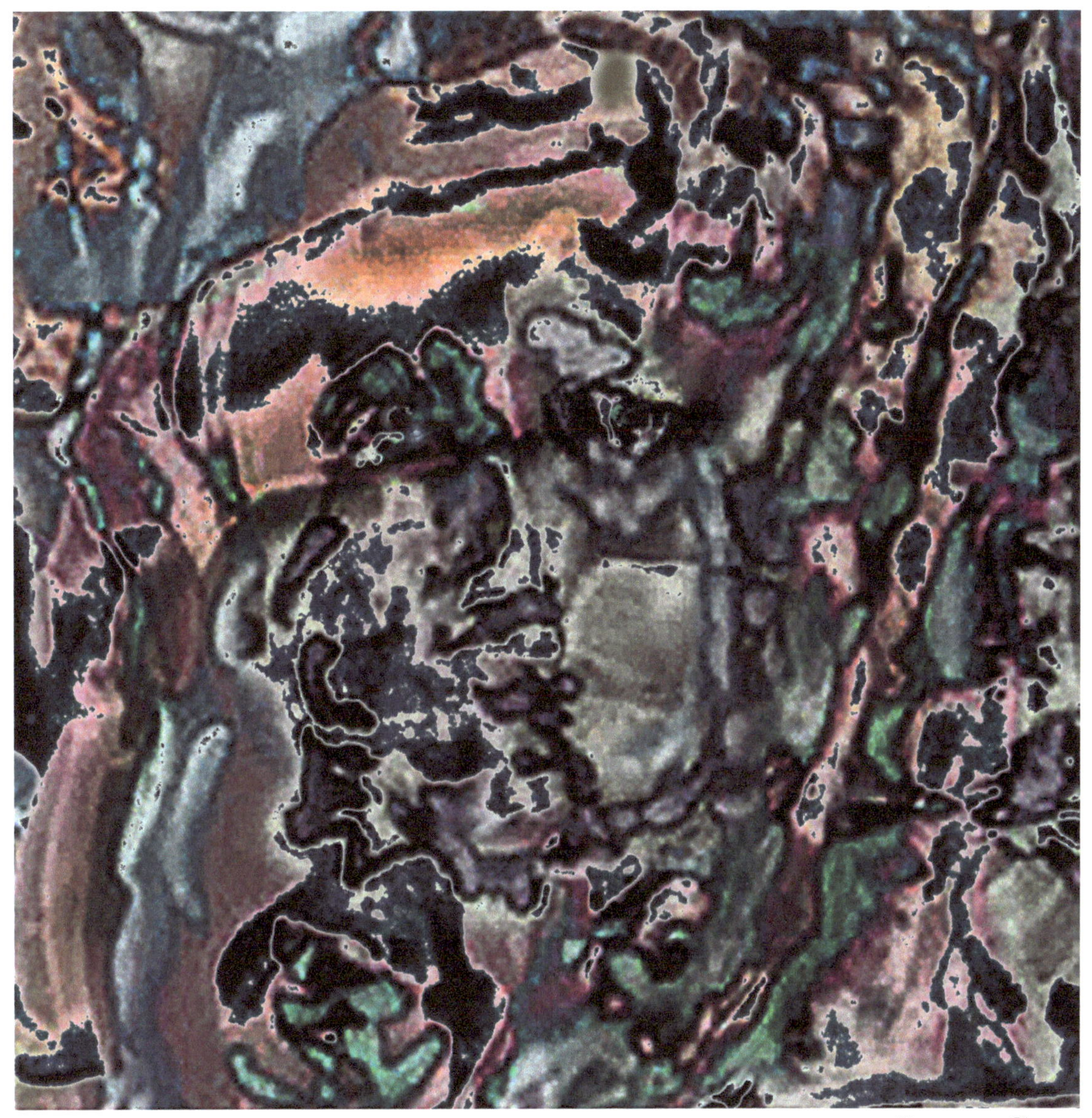

Brain Strain

"Contrary to what everyone knows is so, it may not be the brain that produces consciousness, but rather consciousness that creates the appearance of the brain-matter, space, time, and everything else we are pleased to interpret as the physical universe."
~KEITH FLOYD, psychologist at Virginia Intermont College

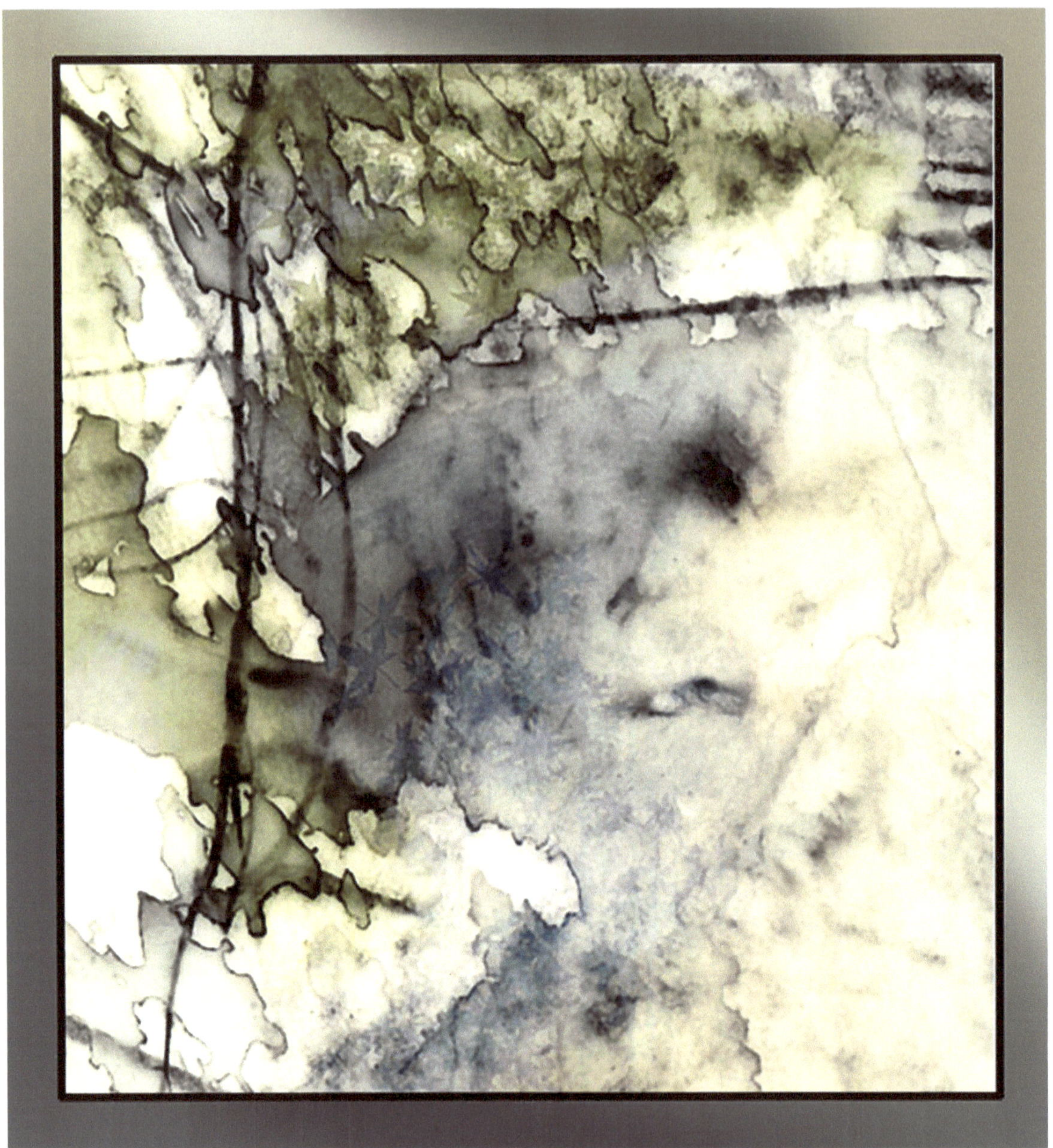

Shy, Could Be a Friend

"We are indeed on a shaman's journey, mere children struggling to become technicians of the sacred."
~MICHAEL TALBOT, The Holographic Universe, 1991

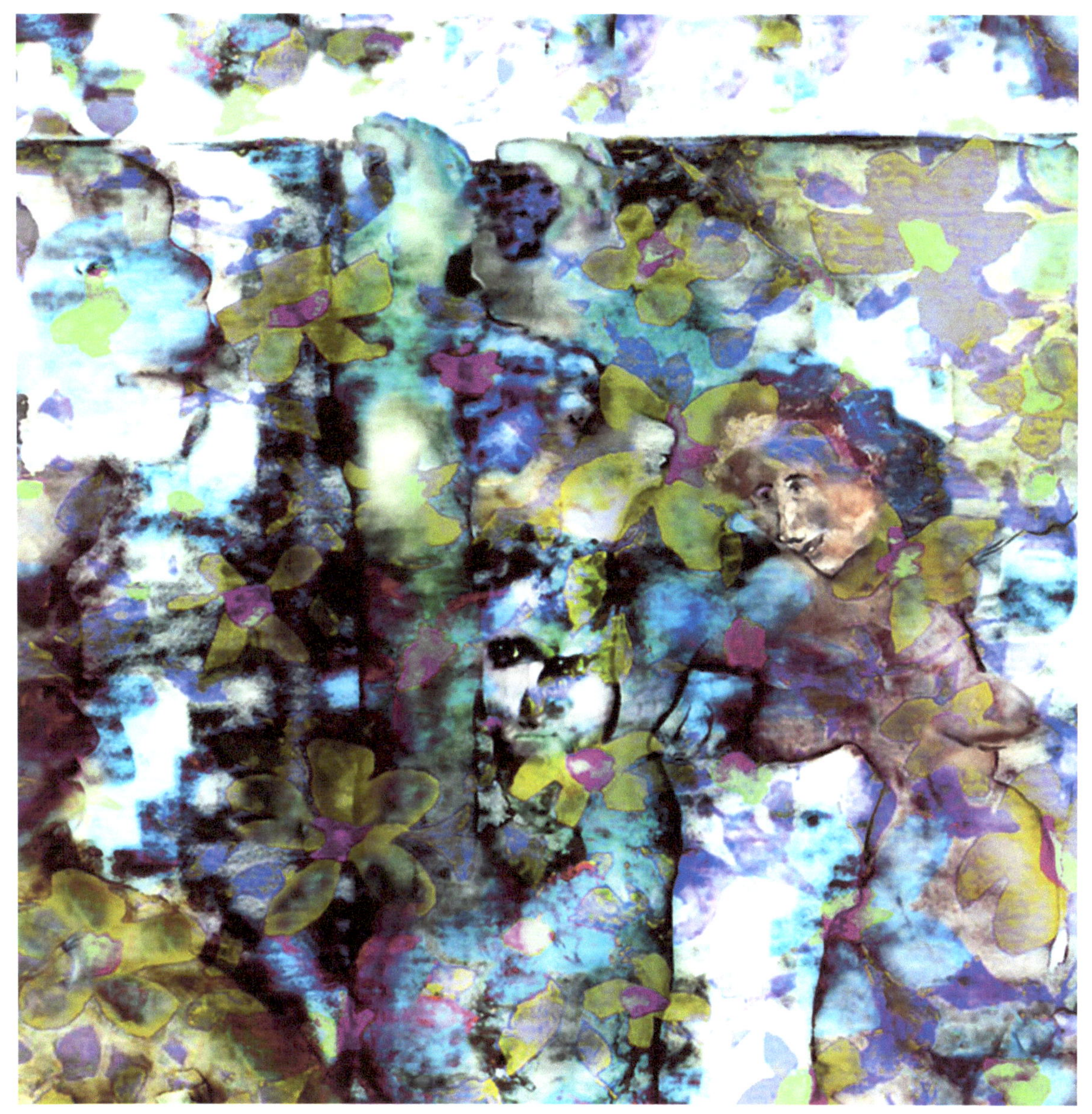

Atlas' World,
Blend, Detail

"Quantum mechanics clearly show that nothing can be predetermined no matter how events may appear. Not only is our world a small world, it is a Zen World after all."
~FRED ALAN WOLF, Taking the Quantum Leap,1981

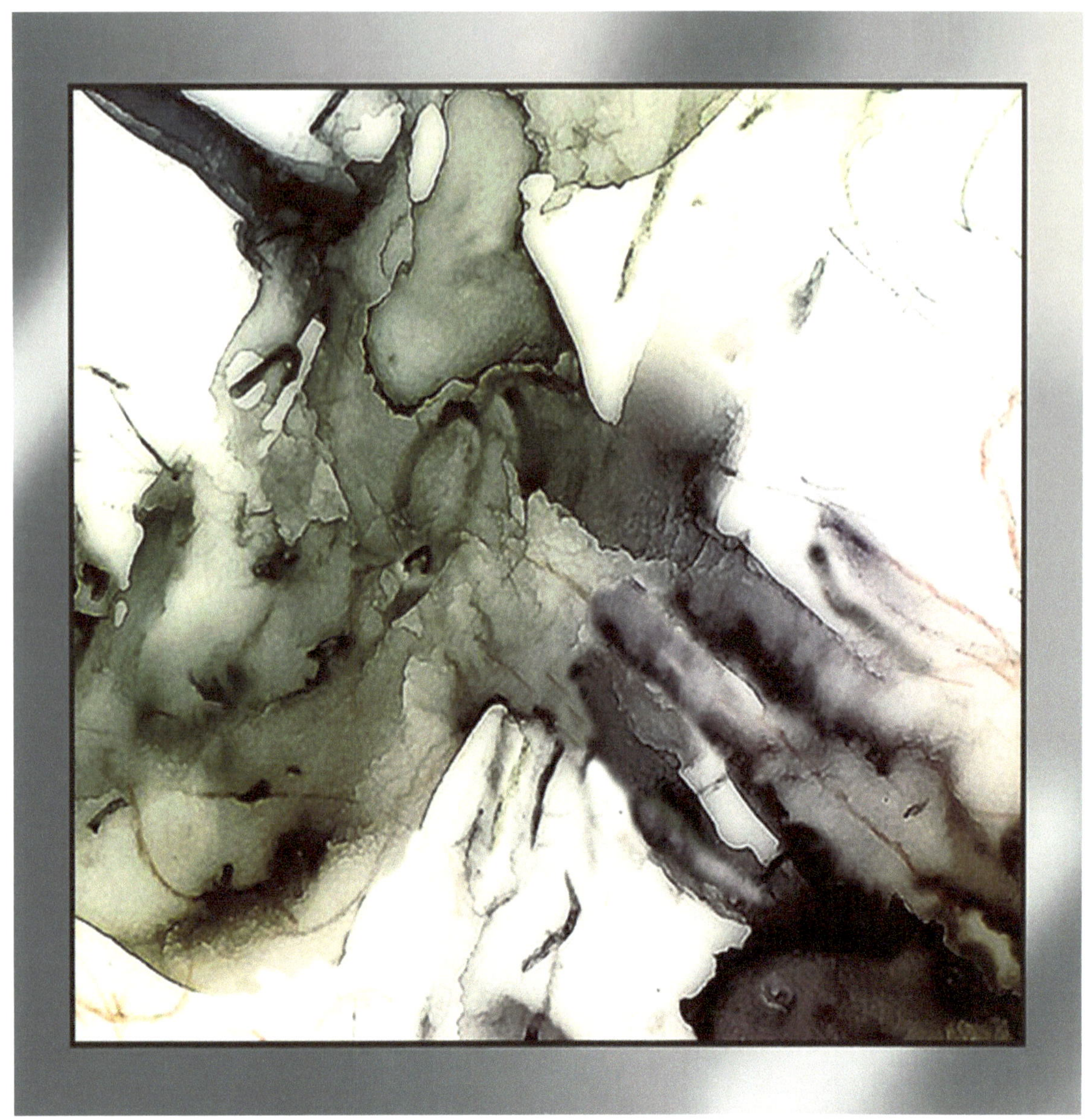

Elusive Self-Esteem

"The highest form of human intelligence is
to observe yourself without judgement."
~KRISHNAMURTI

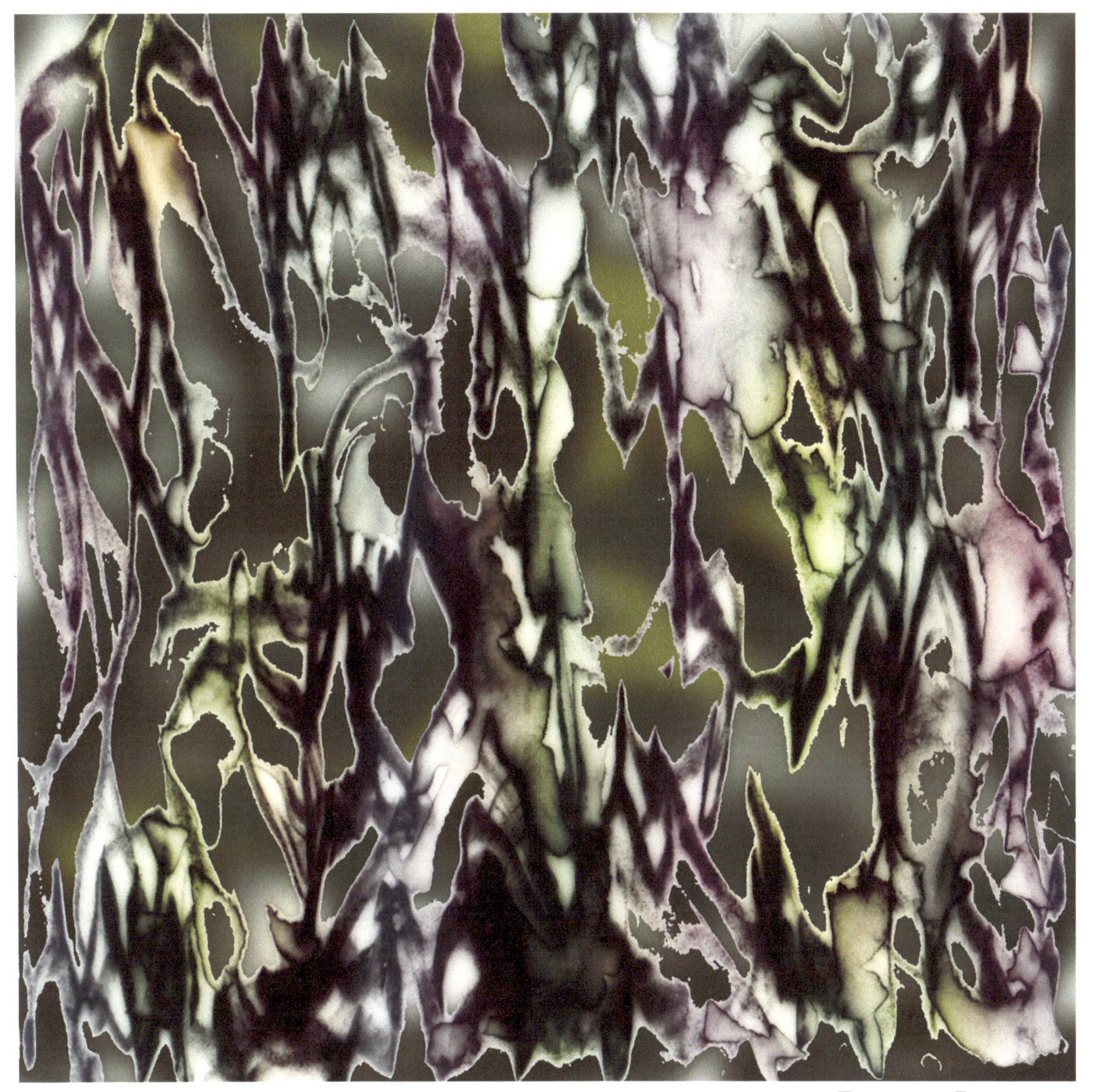

Dance Insanity 2

"When you achieve self-realization, you no longer identify with your body, mind, ego, or desires. You become a pure witness and in that state you can choose to transcend karma."
~DEEPAK CHOPRA, Life After Death, 2006,

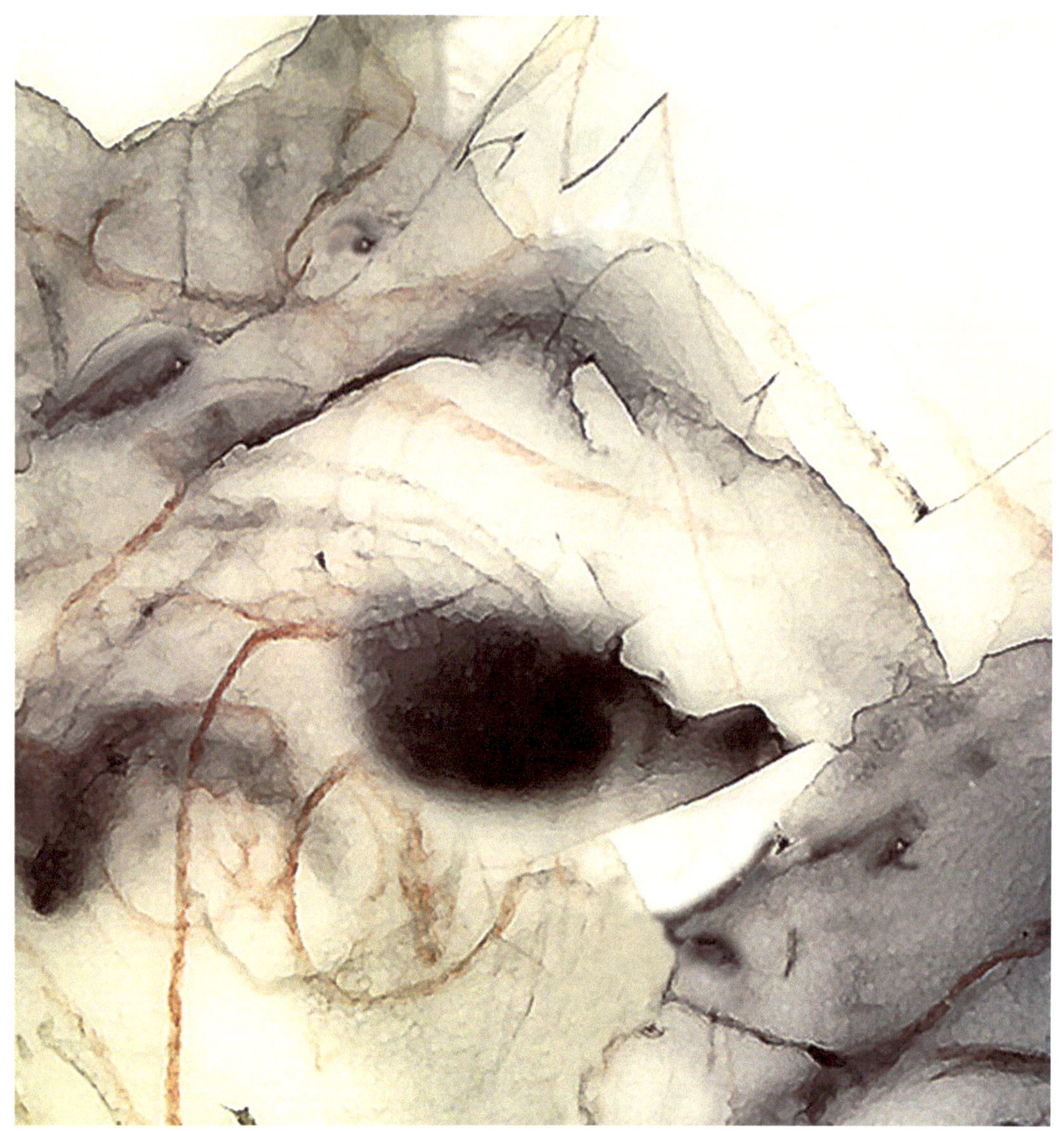

What We See

"Some studies suggest that less than 50 percent of we see is actually based on information entering our eyes. The remaining 50 percent plus is pieced together out of our expectations of what the world should look like...
the eyes may be visual organs, but it is the brain that sees."
~MICHAEL TALBOT - The Holographic Universe. 1991

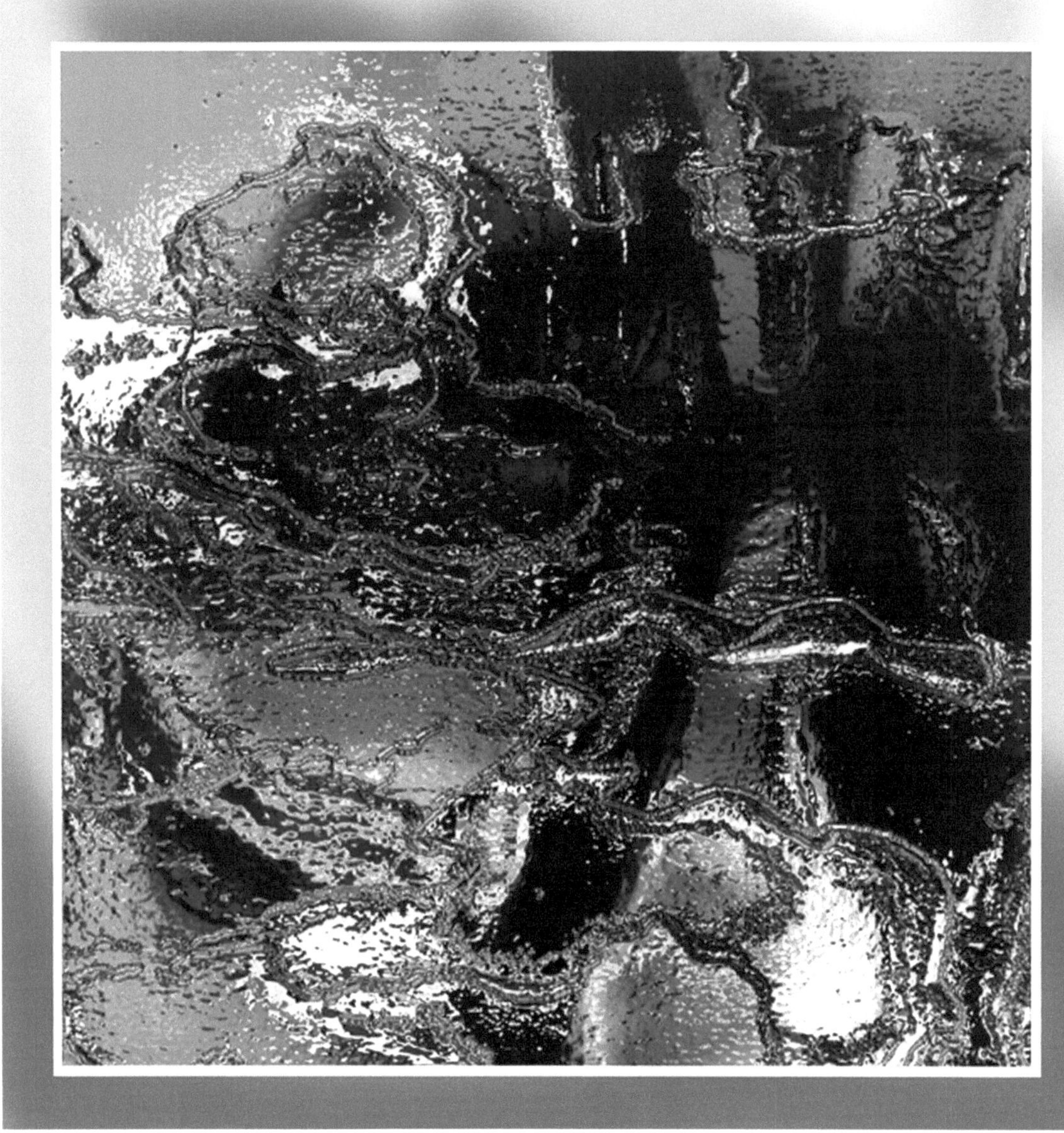

Magma of the Unconscious Mind

"Heaven and hell are recent concepts in human history; hell is not in the old Testament."
~Mellen-Thomas, Messages from the Light

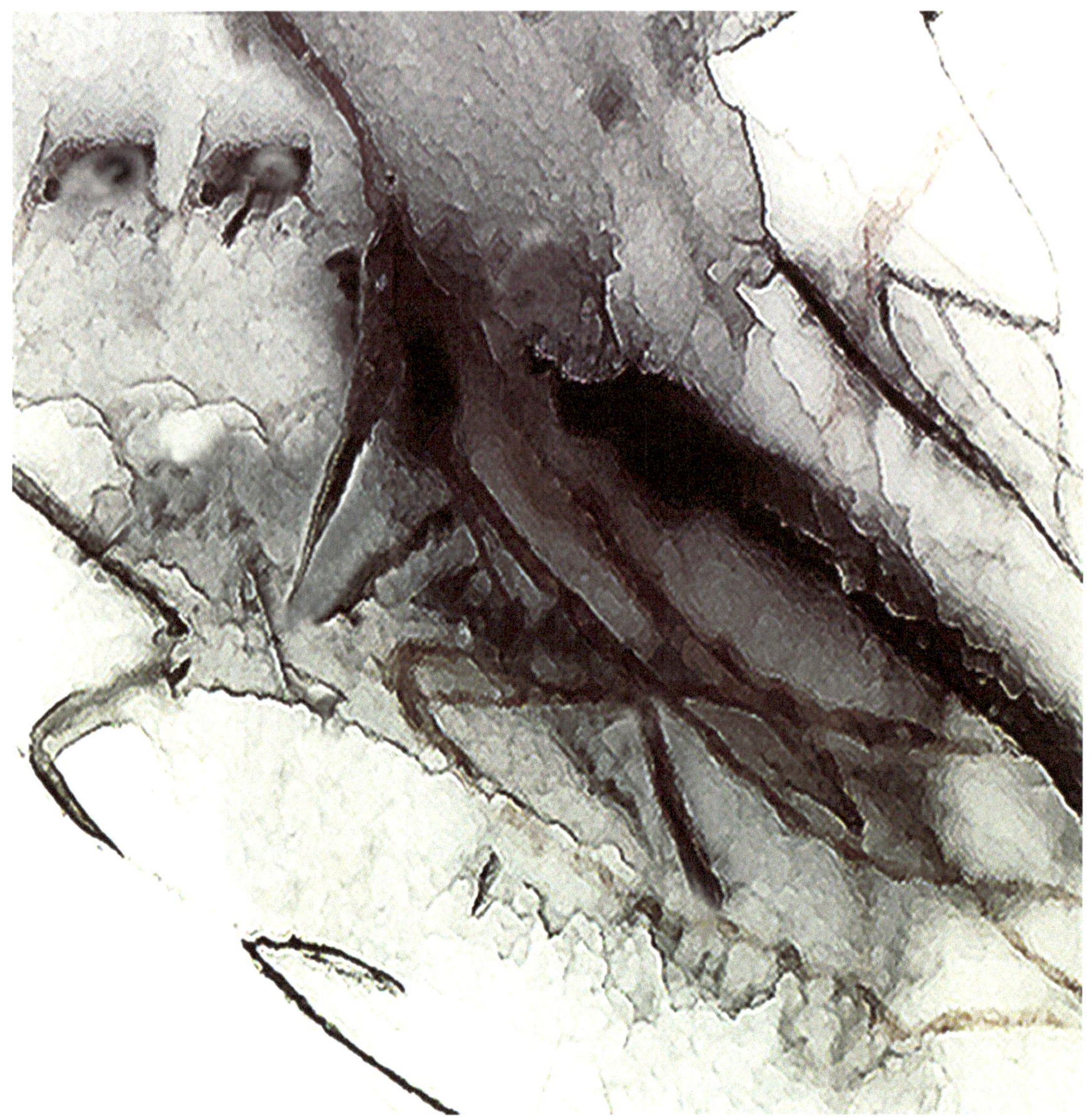

The Great & Mighty Mosquito

"The great and mighty mosquito, to this day, kills and ravishes human beings and animals more than all the human wars on earth. If you check World Health, to this day it's still the biggest killer of humanity."
~Mellen-Thomas, Messages from the Light

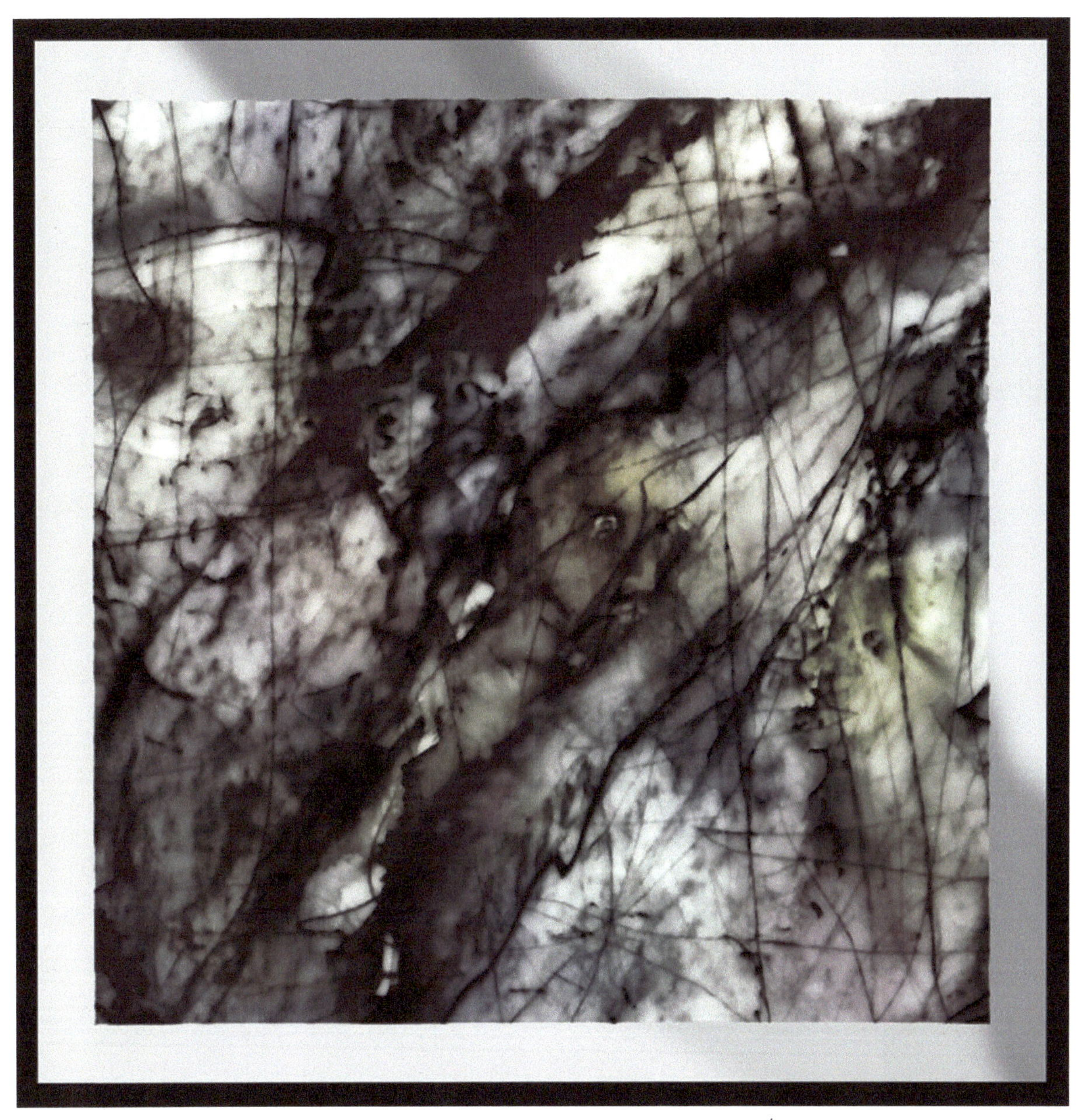

Awareness,
the Source of All That Is

"We are made from star-dust, in creation and re-creation. It is incredibly mystical and magical."
~Mellen-Thomas, Messages from the Light

Masquerade

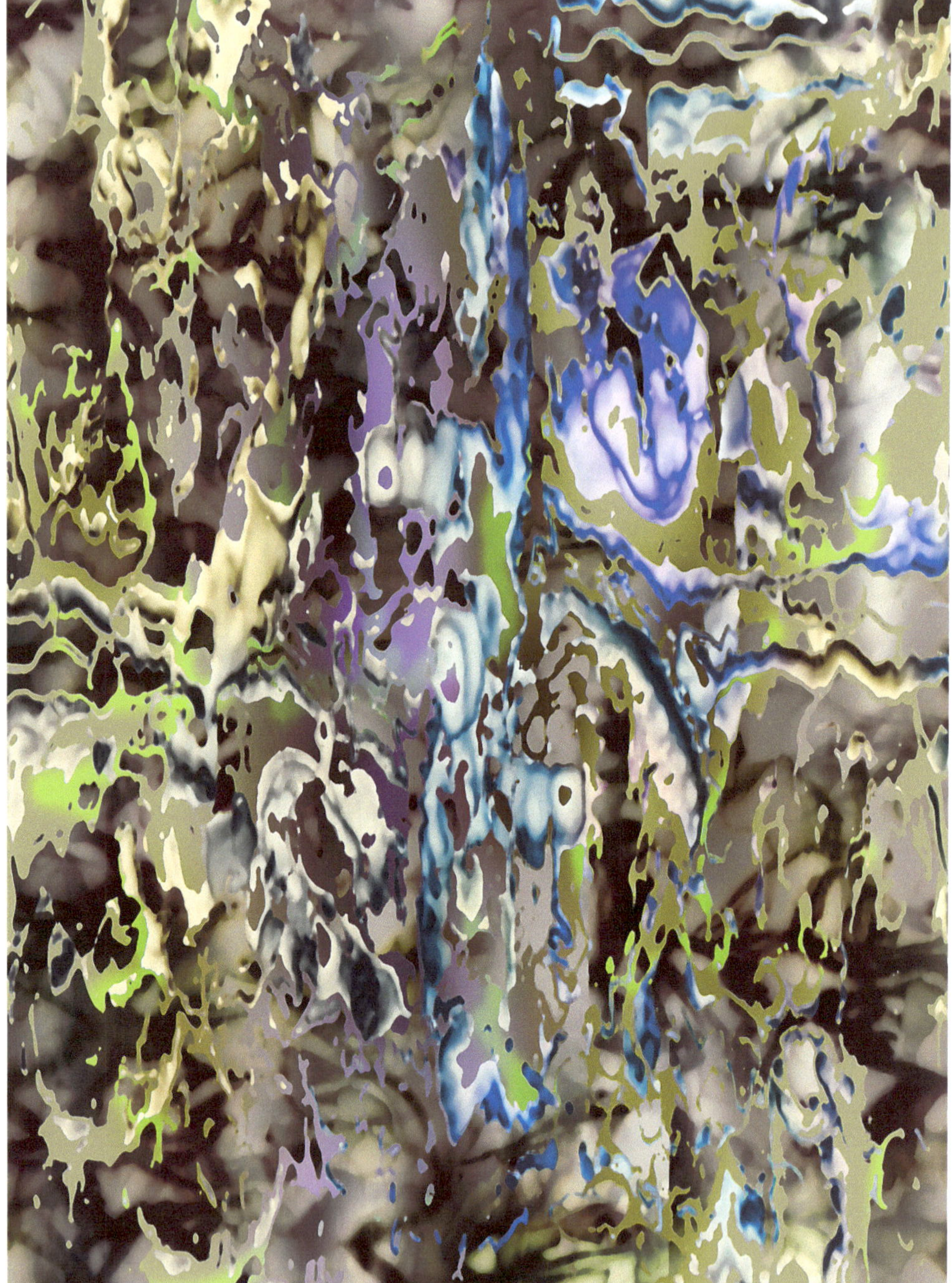

"Free energy is a
metaphor for free spirit.
When the time
is right for an idea,
nothing can suppress it."
~Mellen-Thomas,
Messages from the Light

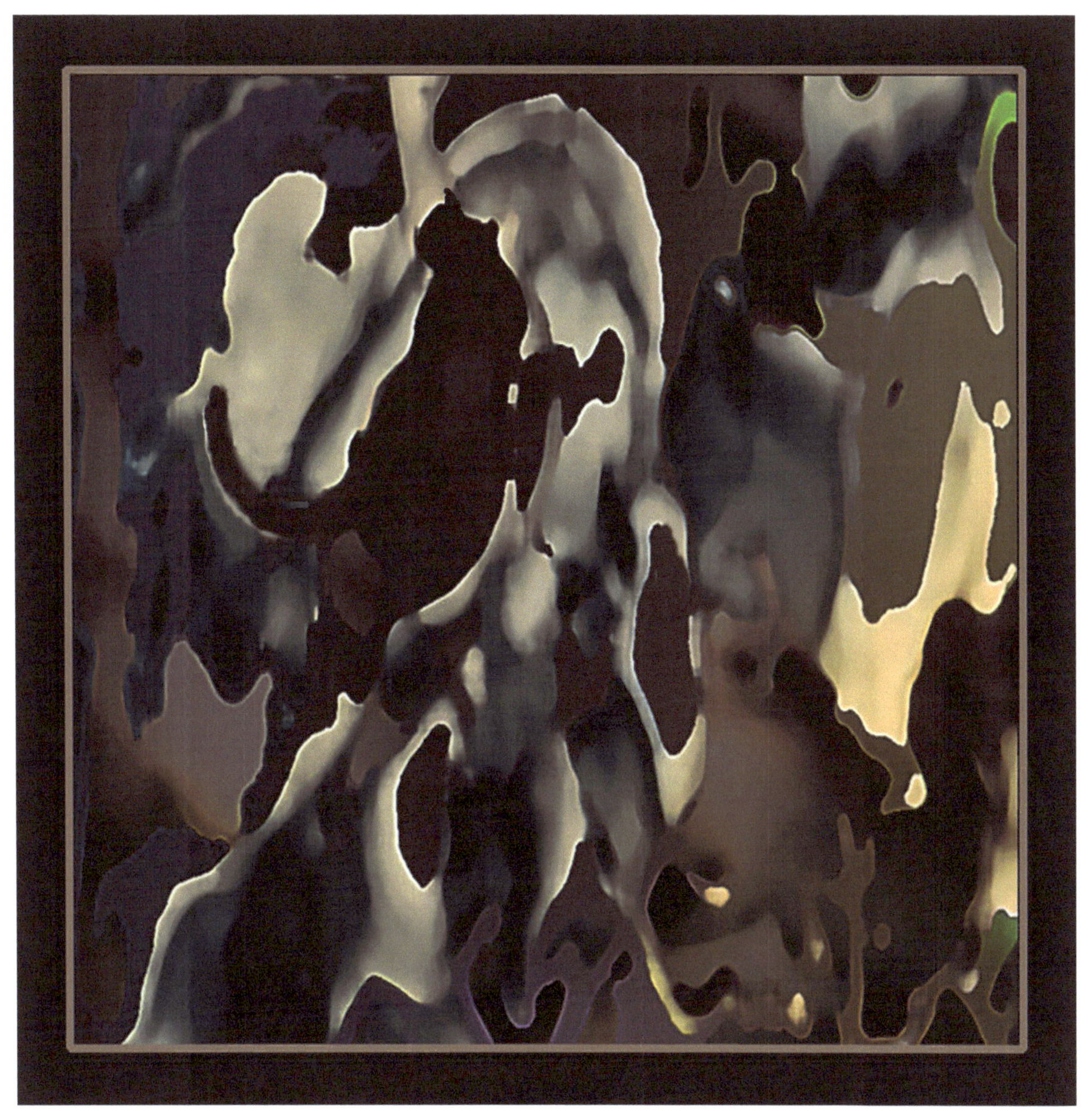

Reincarnation

"Spiritual new age explanations of reincarnation are flimsy but the Quantum Physics, the Quantum Mechanics are solid. This will be a science in the future. The Quantum nature of the reality of reincarnation is more real and more dynamic than people image"

~Mellen-Thomas, Messages from the Light

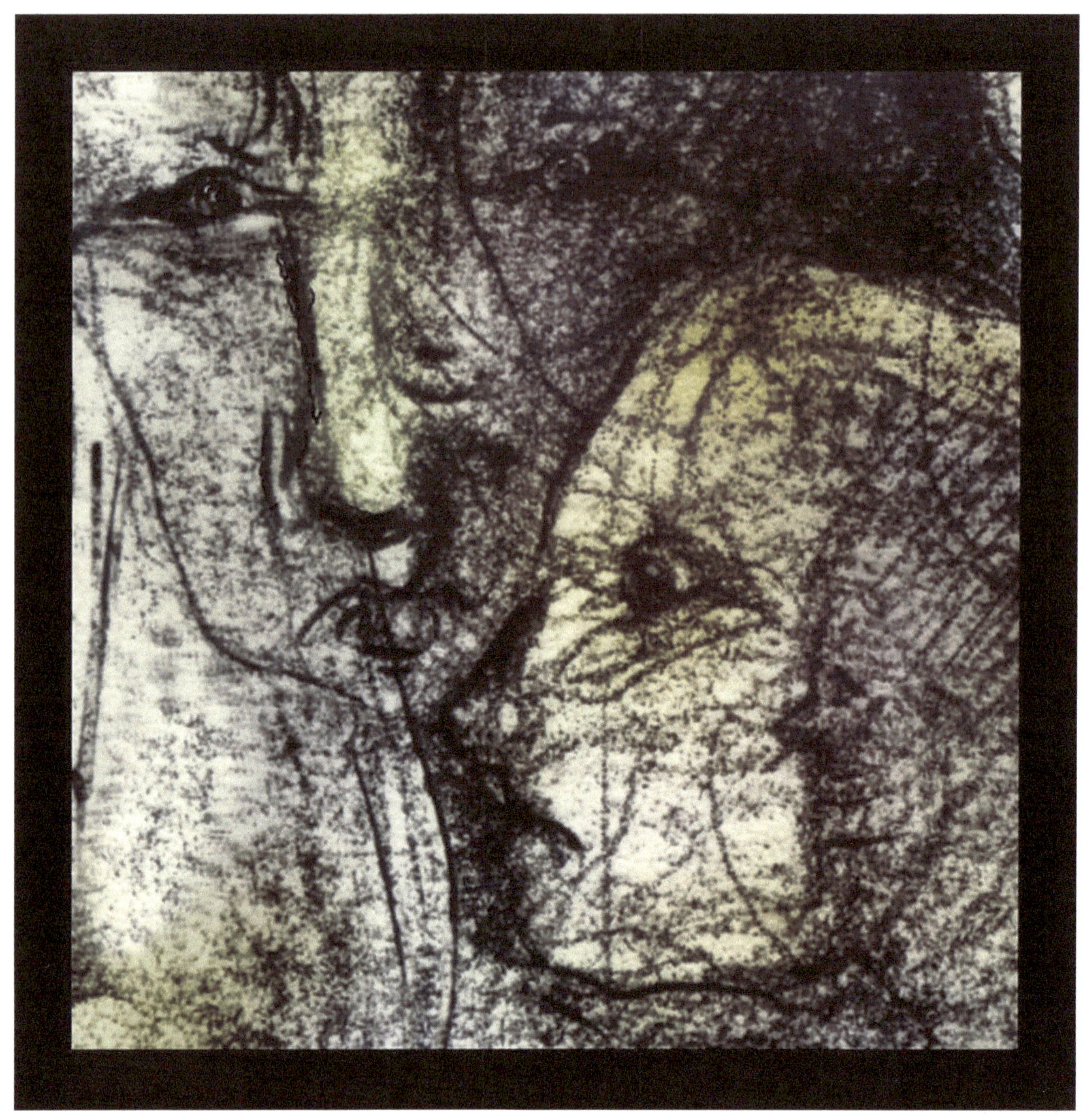

Ambivalence, Detail

"We are not human beings having
a spiritual experience. We are spiritual
beings having a human experience."
~Pierre Teilhard de Chardin.

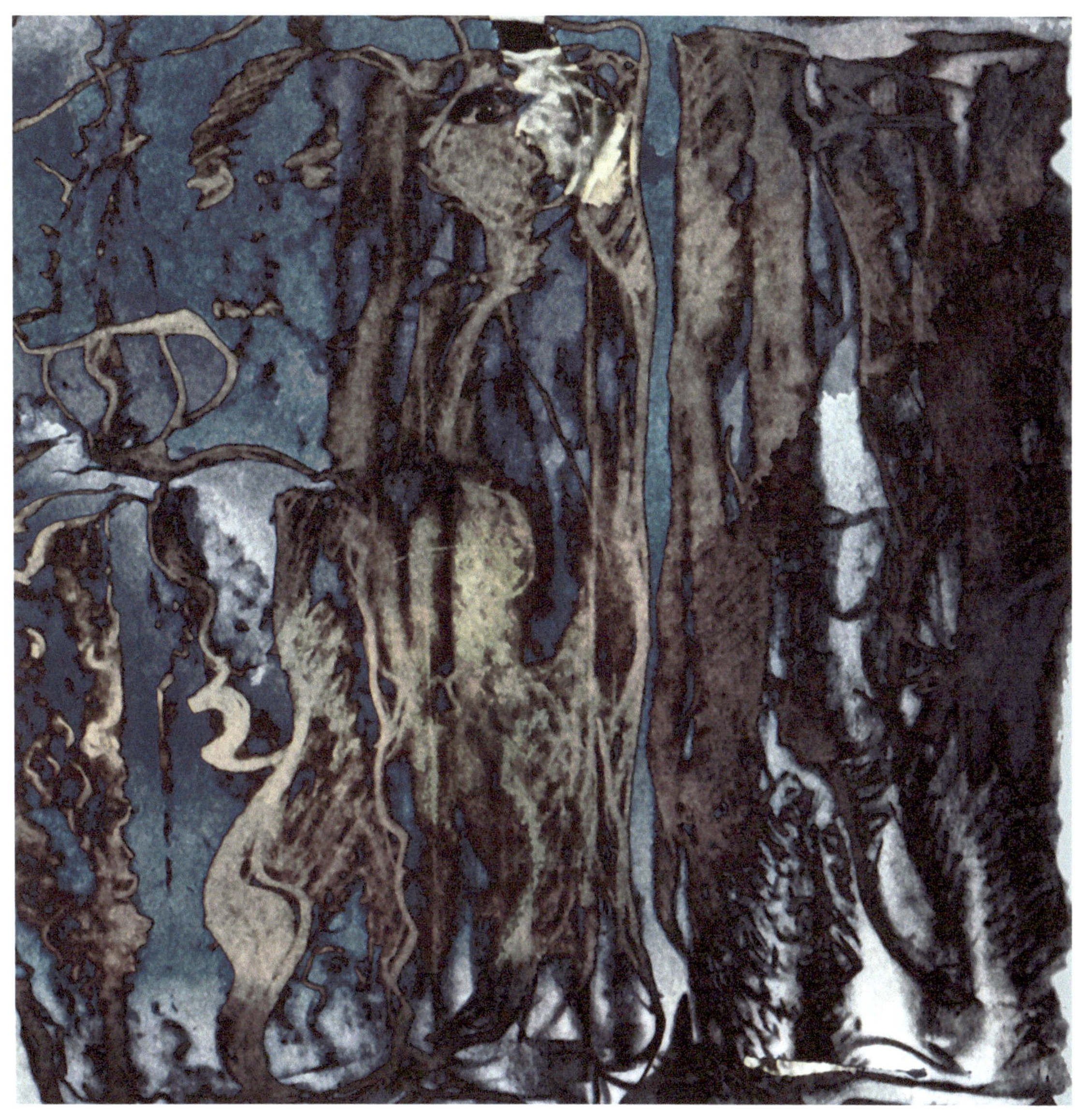

Plantae

"Plants have feelings. A plant never lies.
Shamans have spoken with plants
...a plant tells you what it's good for."
~Mellen-Thomas re: Clive Backster, Primary Perception

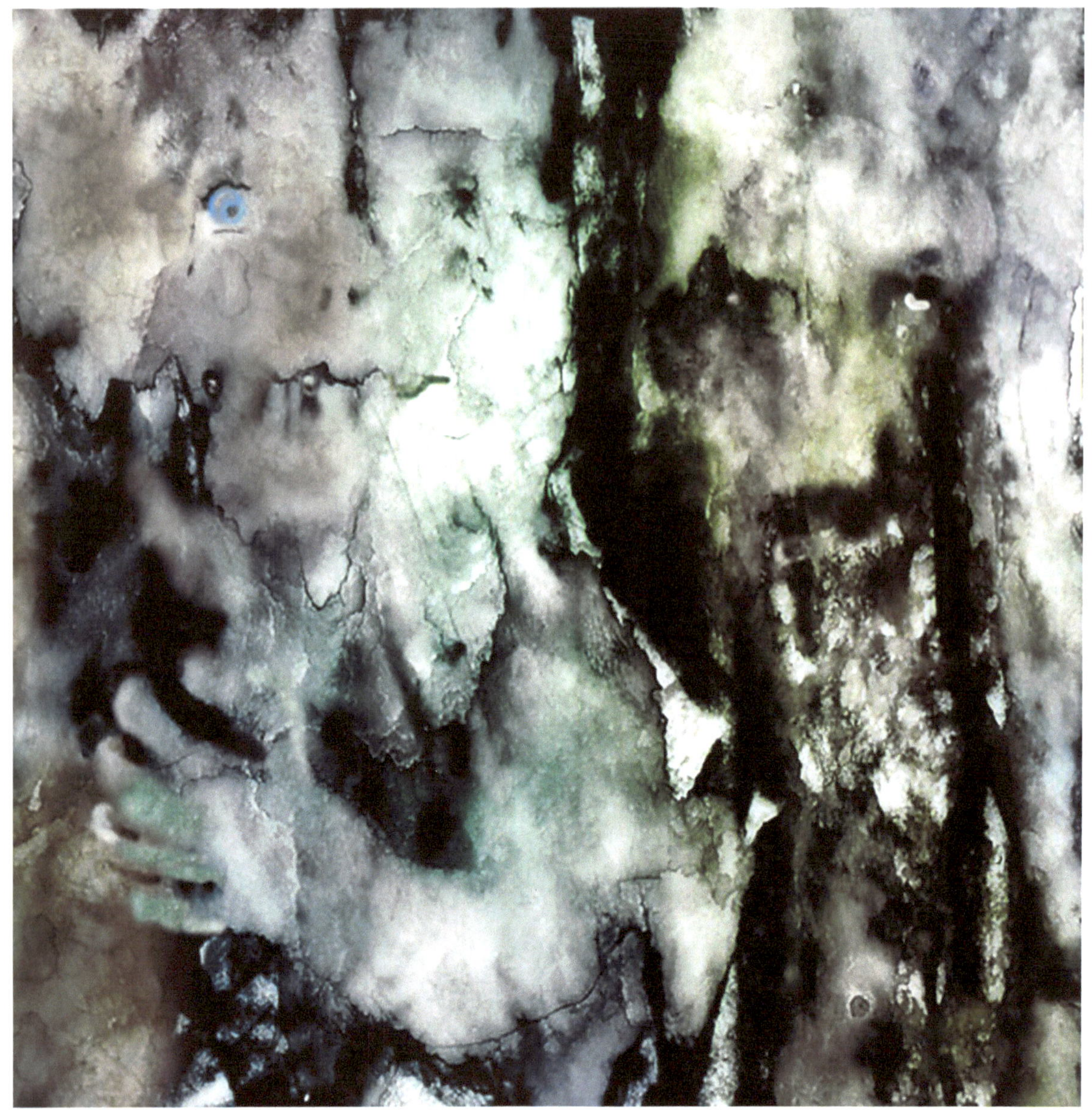

Forest Friends, Detail 3

"2012 is not the end of the world but a cosmological signpost. Reincarnation is more real and dynamic than people can imagine."
~Mellen-Thomas, Messages from the Light

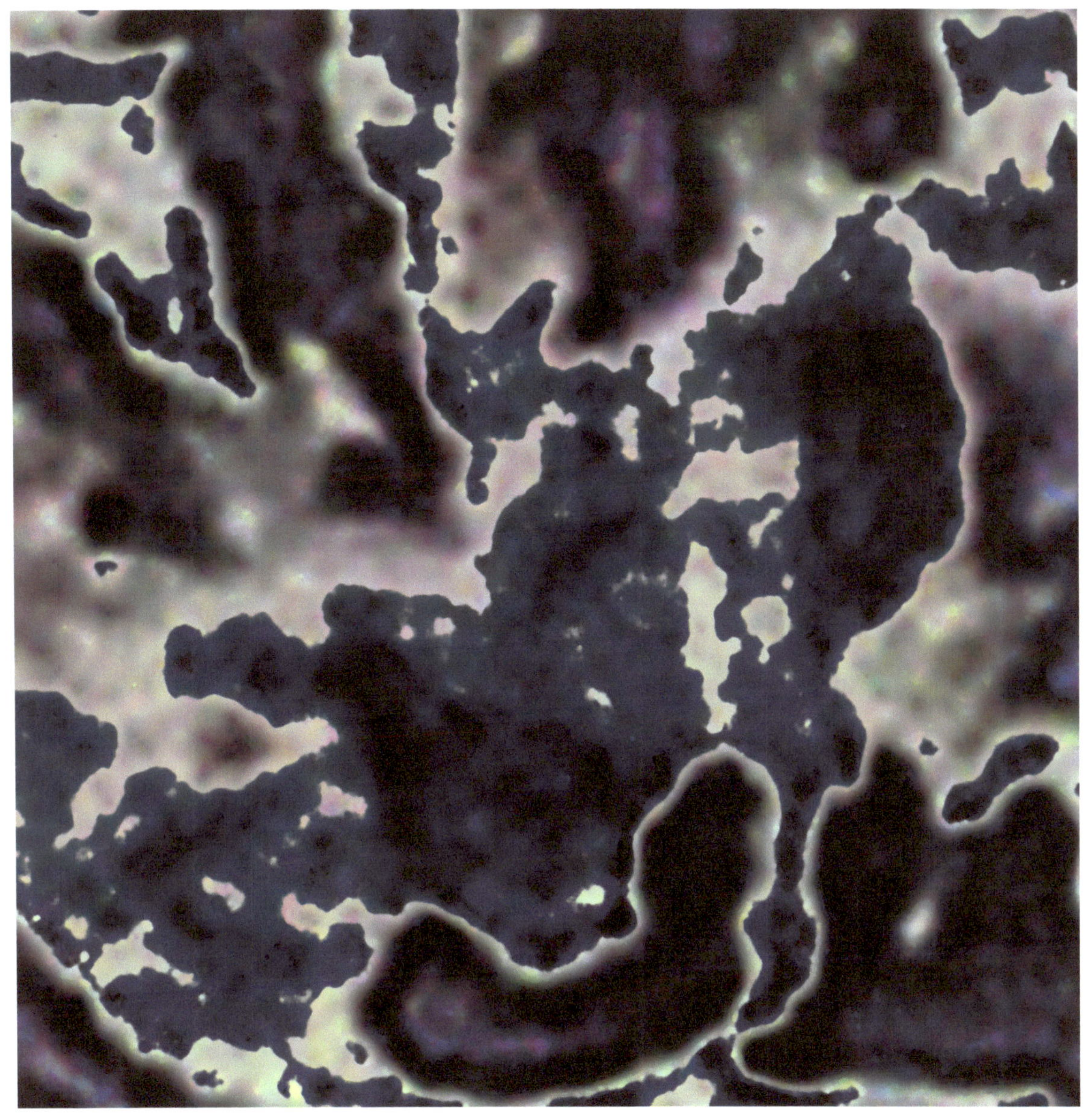

The Fragmented Mind

"Can a fragmented mind
ever experience Wholeness?"
~KRISHNAMURTI

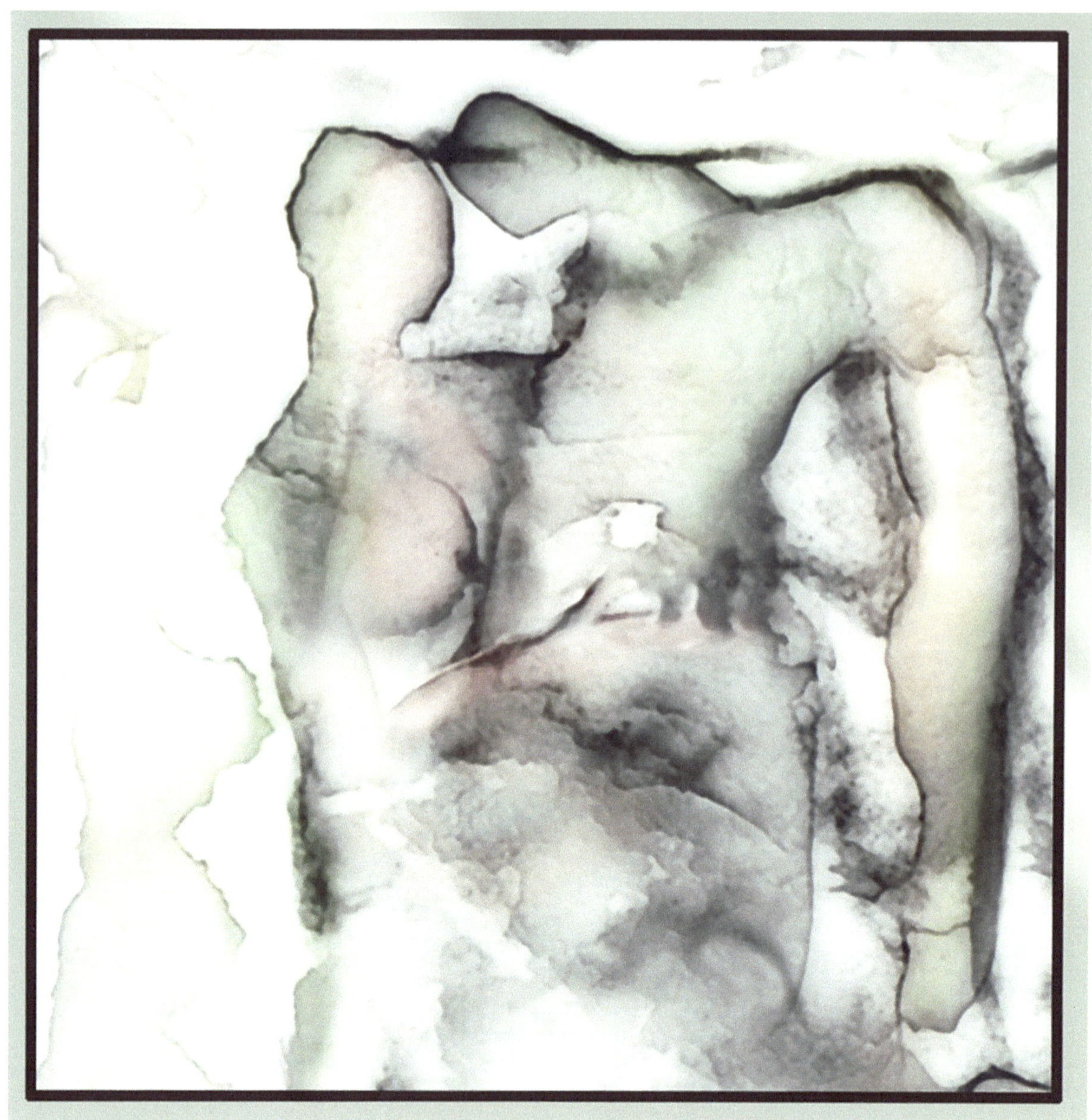

Lovers in the Sky

"Look again...for deep in every human soul there is a knowing that all life is a gift beyond measure. And that love, yes love is the heart and the breath and the meaning of life." *~Invocation of Ecstasy...a poem by Mellen-Thomas*

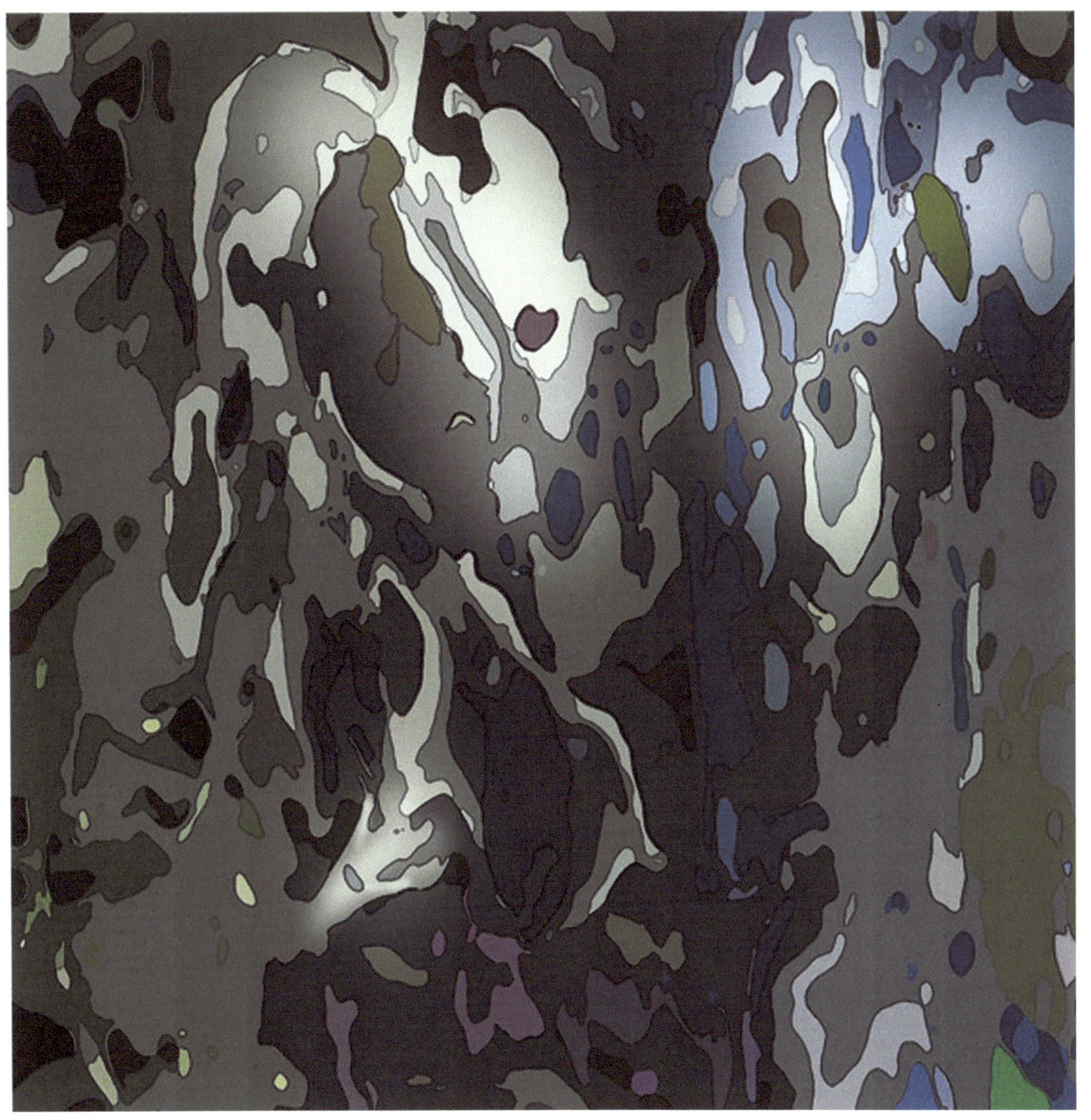

Folding Back In On Myself

"Folding back in on myself,
I create again and again."
~KRISHNA in the Bhagavah-Gita

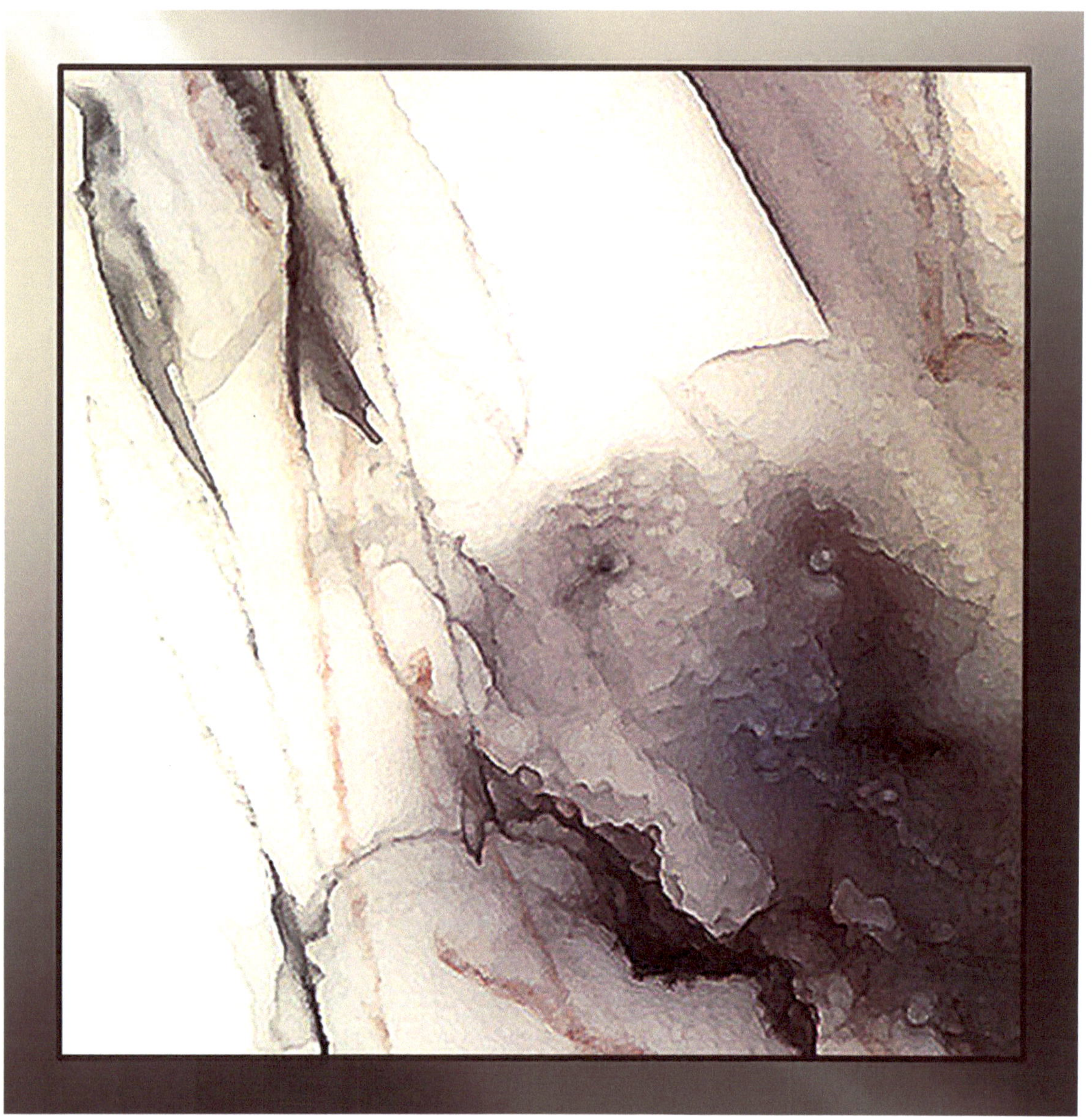

File Keeper

"Spontaneous regeneration happens in every know human condition. What is the physics of this? Because if it really happens in flesh there is a science behind it we need to understand."

~Mellen-Thomas, Messages from the Light

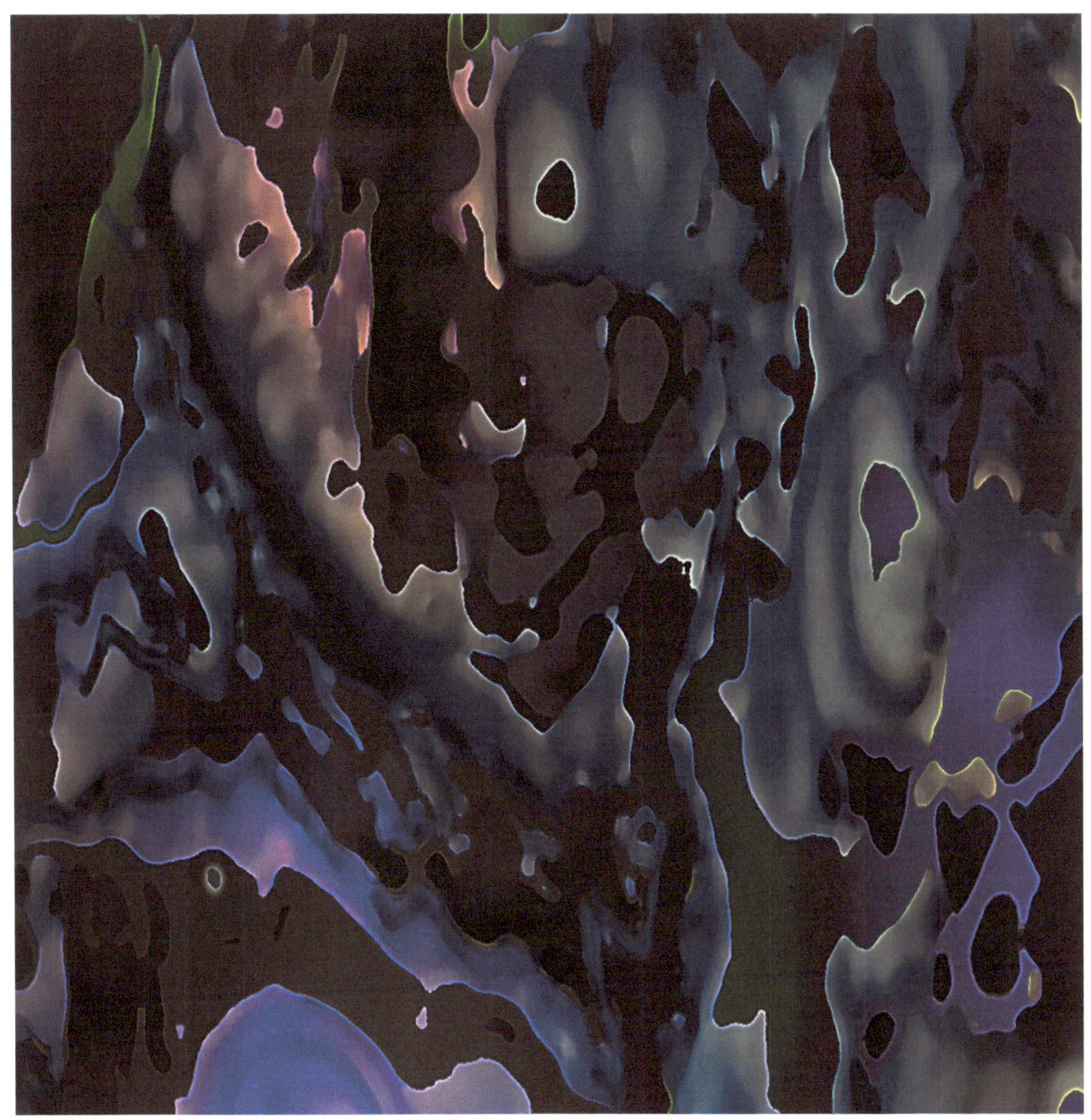

A Hologram of Energy

"Quantum physics now scientifically supports ...that everything from our material bodies to our experiences to our planet to our universe form a seamless hologram of energy."
~Mellen-Thomas, Messages from the Light

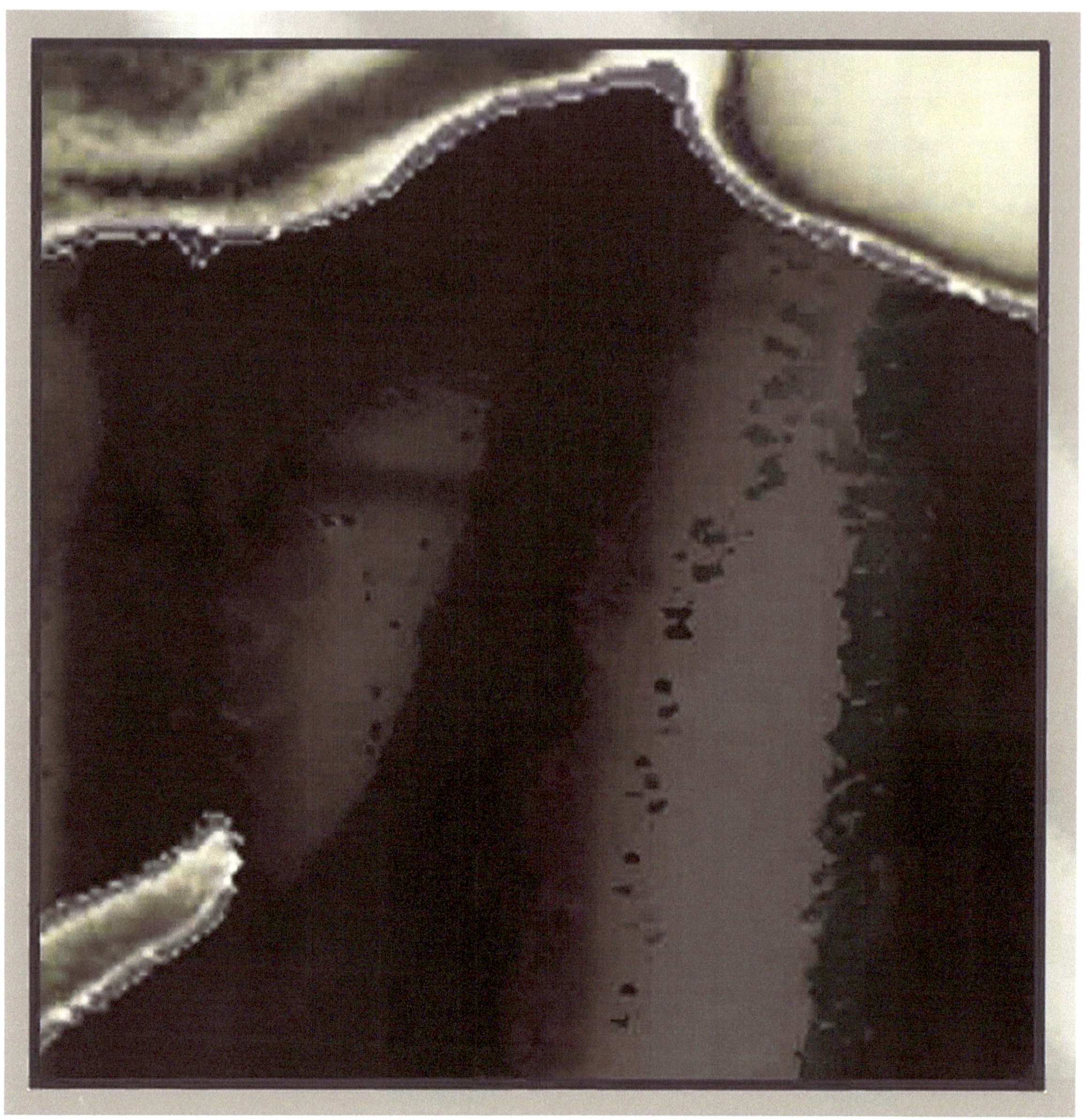

Regeneration

"Everything about us is magical...even the universe. Everything we see is impossible. Yet here we are."
~Mellen-Thomas, Messages from the Light

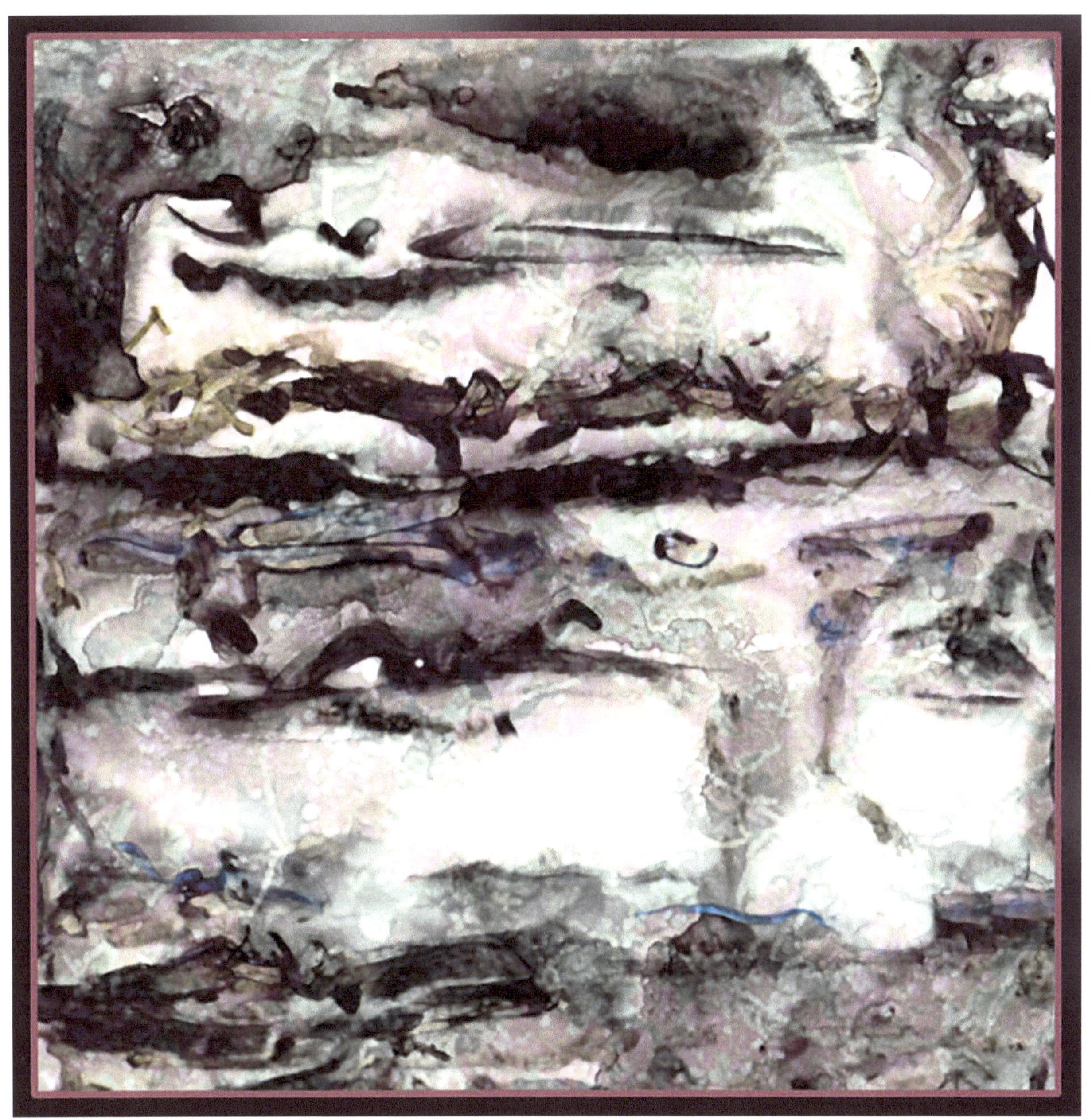

Possibility

"I dwell in possibility."
~EMILY DICKINSON

Complements of the Cosmic House

"Physicists have discovered that with our physical universe, or 'cosmic house' there are two different ways of observing it.
We can view the universe in terms of particles, or we can view it as made up of waves. These two ways of seeing are complementary to each other; that is, we cannot see the universe both ways at the same time. I call these ways "Complements of the Cosmic House."

~FRED ALAN WOLF,

Taking the Quantum Leap,1981/89

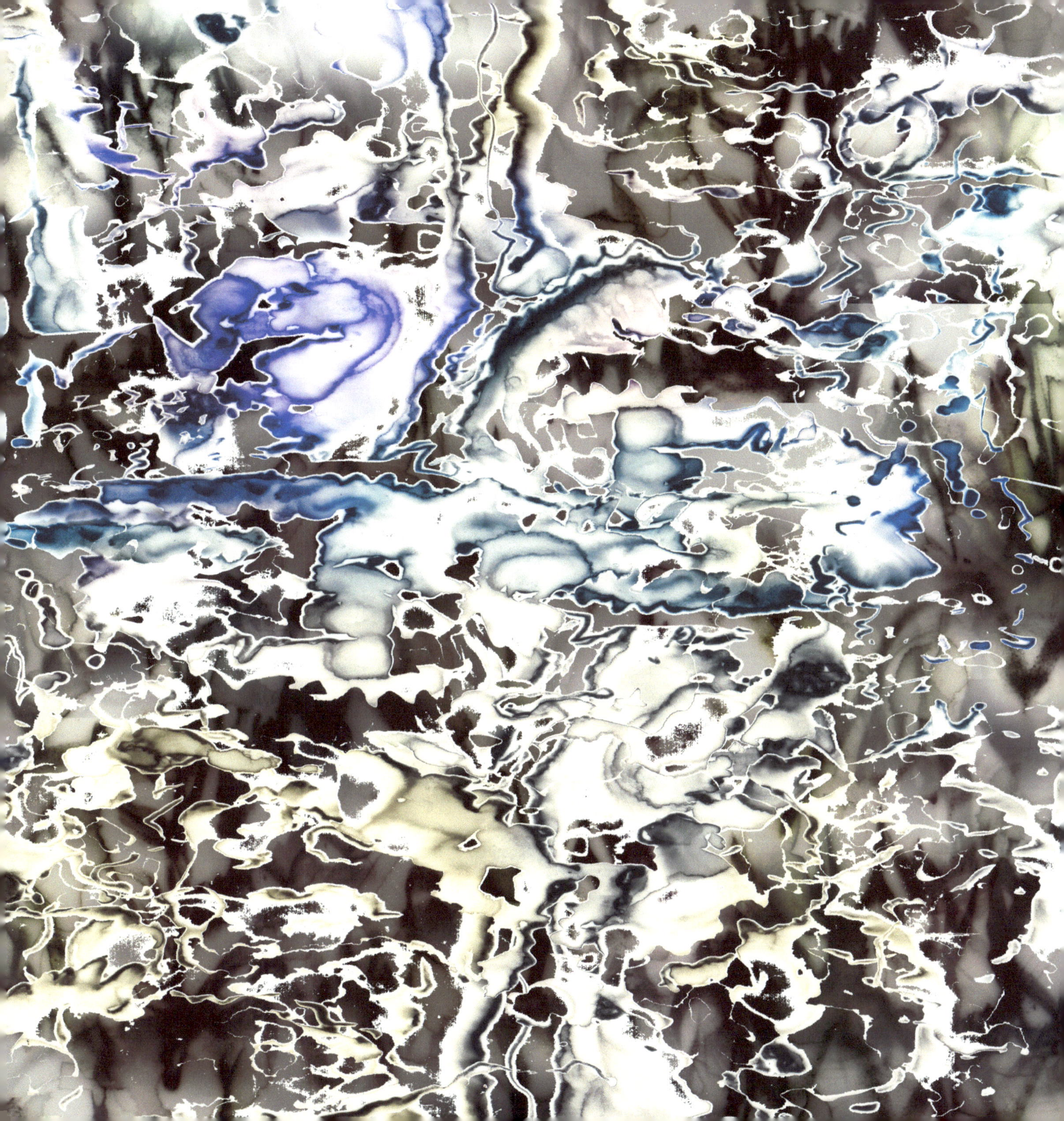

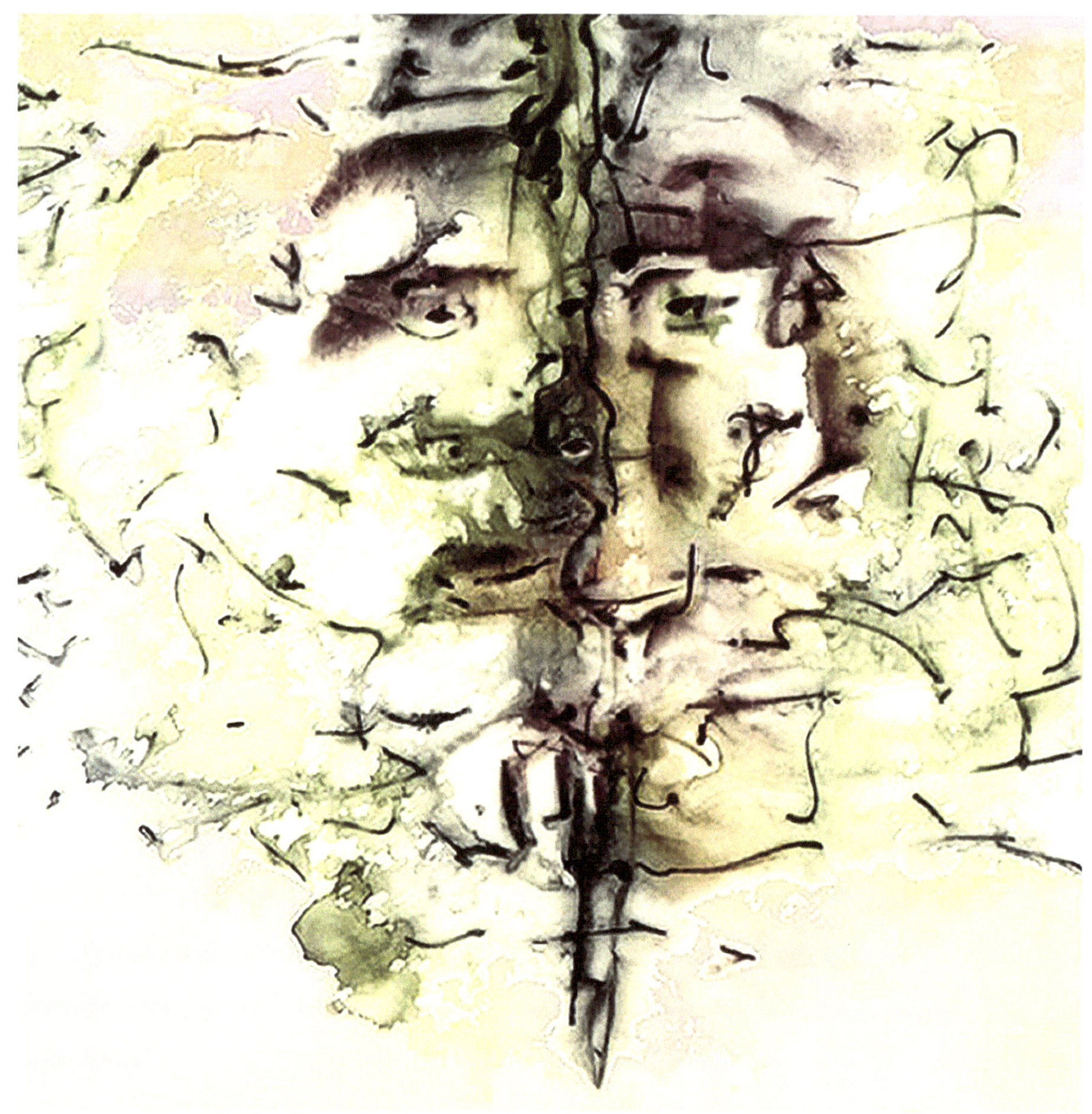

Her Way

"...one of the basic tenants of quantum physics is that we are not discovering reality, but participating in its creation."
~MICHAEL TALBOT - The Holographic Universe, 1991

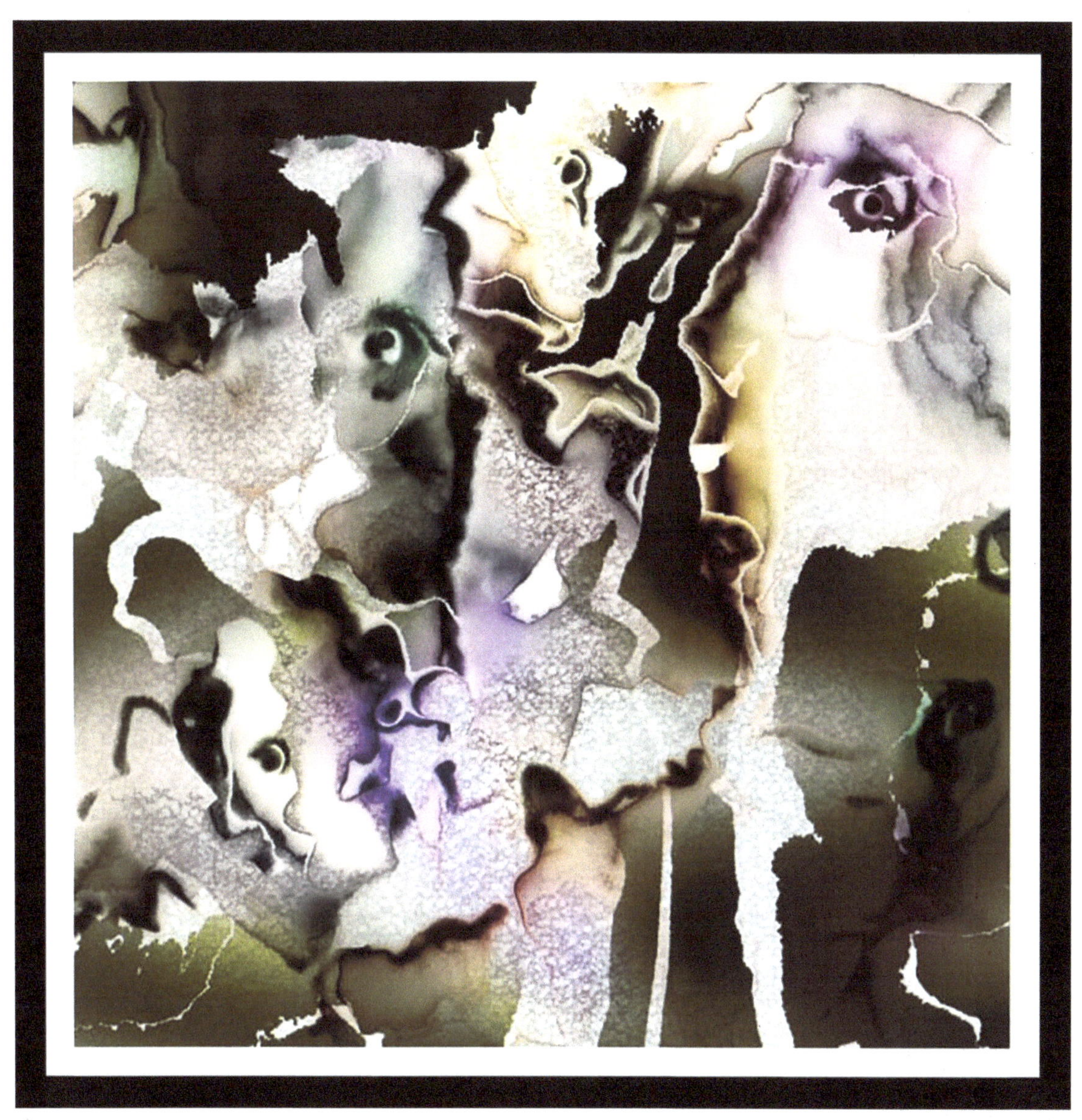

Allowing What Is

"When witnessing the mind...you will just be aware, present, conscious; either witnessing the mind without labelling what you observe or withdrawing awareness and residing in your own stillness."
~http://www.yoga-mind-control.com

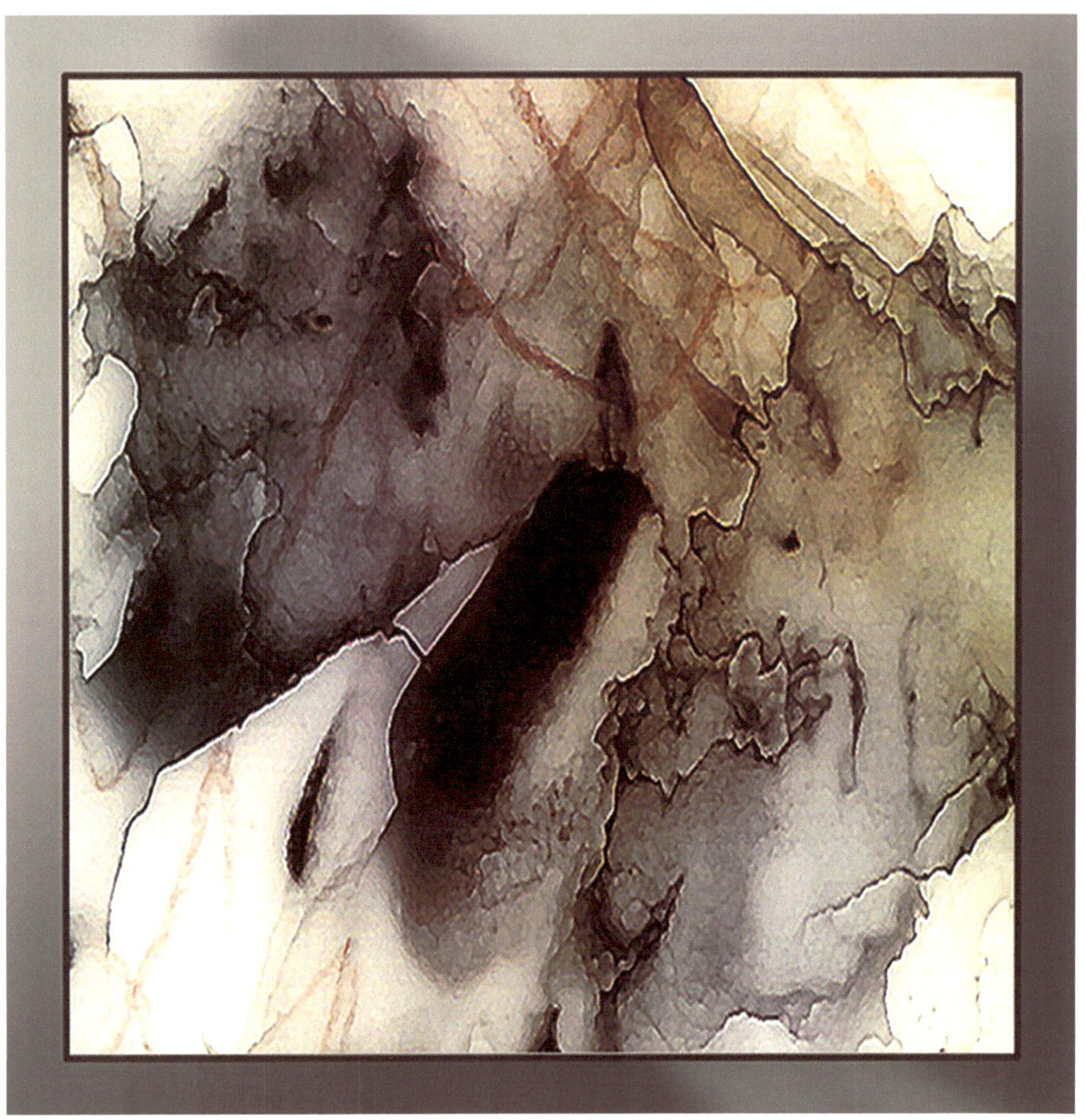

Kiss The Fading Day

"The night kissed the fading day with
a whisper.I am death, your mother.
From me you will get new birth." ~TAGORE

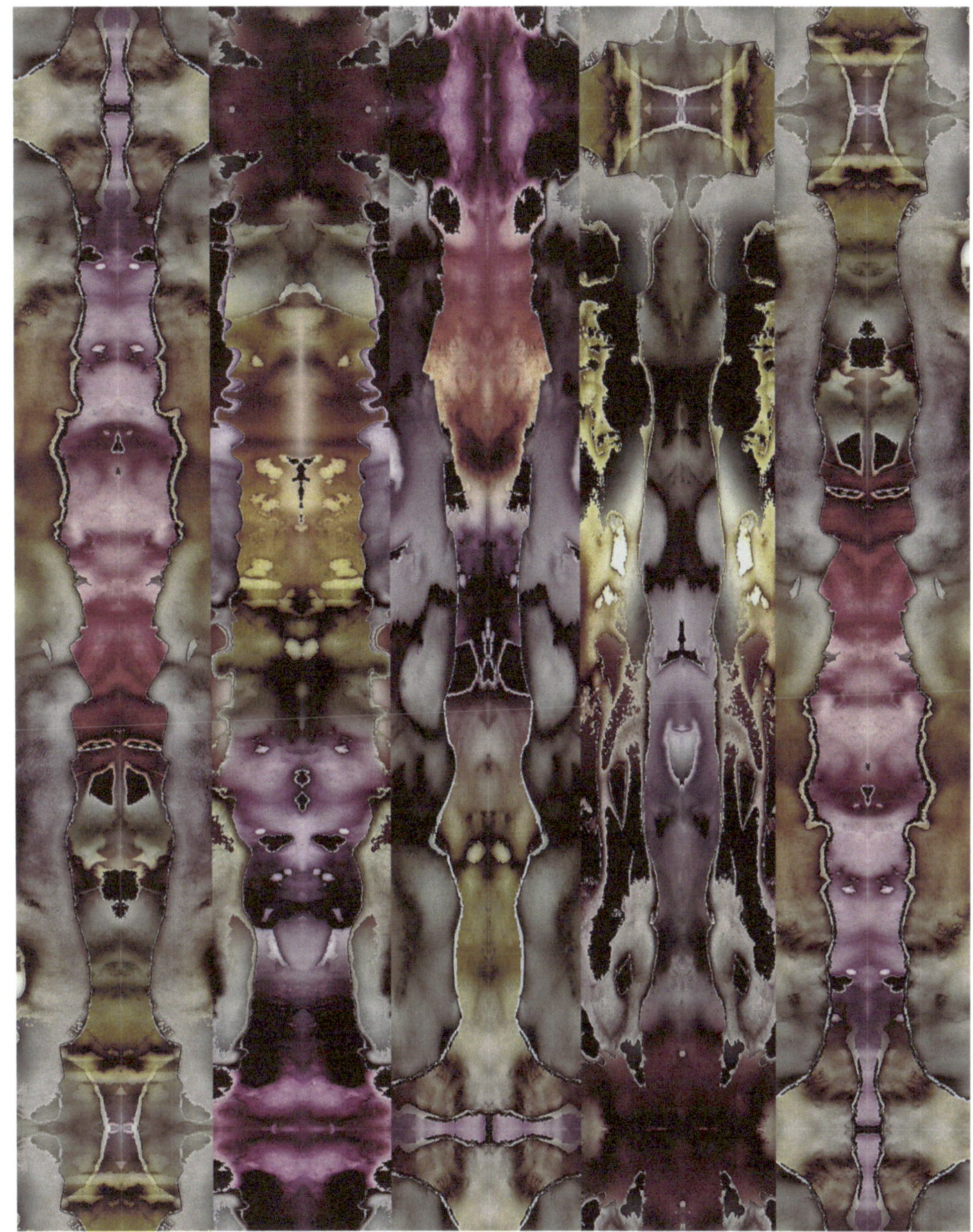

DoppelGanger, Totem

"Indeed, if the universe is a holodeck...all permanence would have to be looked at as illusory, and only consciousness would be eternal, the consciousness of the living universe."
~MICHAEL TALBOT - The Holographic Universe, 1991

Forgiveness is Freeing

"I asked the Light
'Why are humans
so dark and evil?'
The Light turned into a
mandala of human souls,
like a cathedral window.
I saw no evil whatsoever."
~Mellen-Thomas,
Messages from the Light

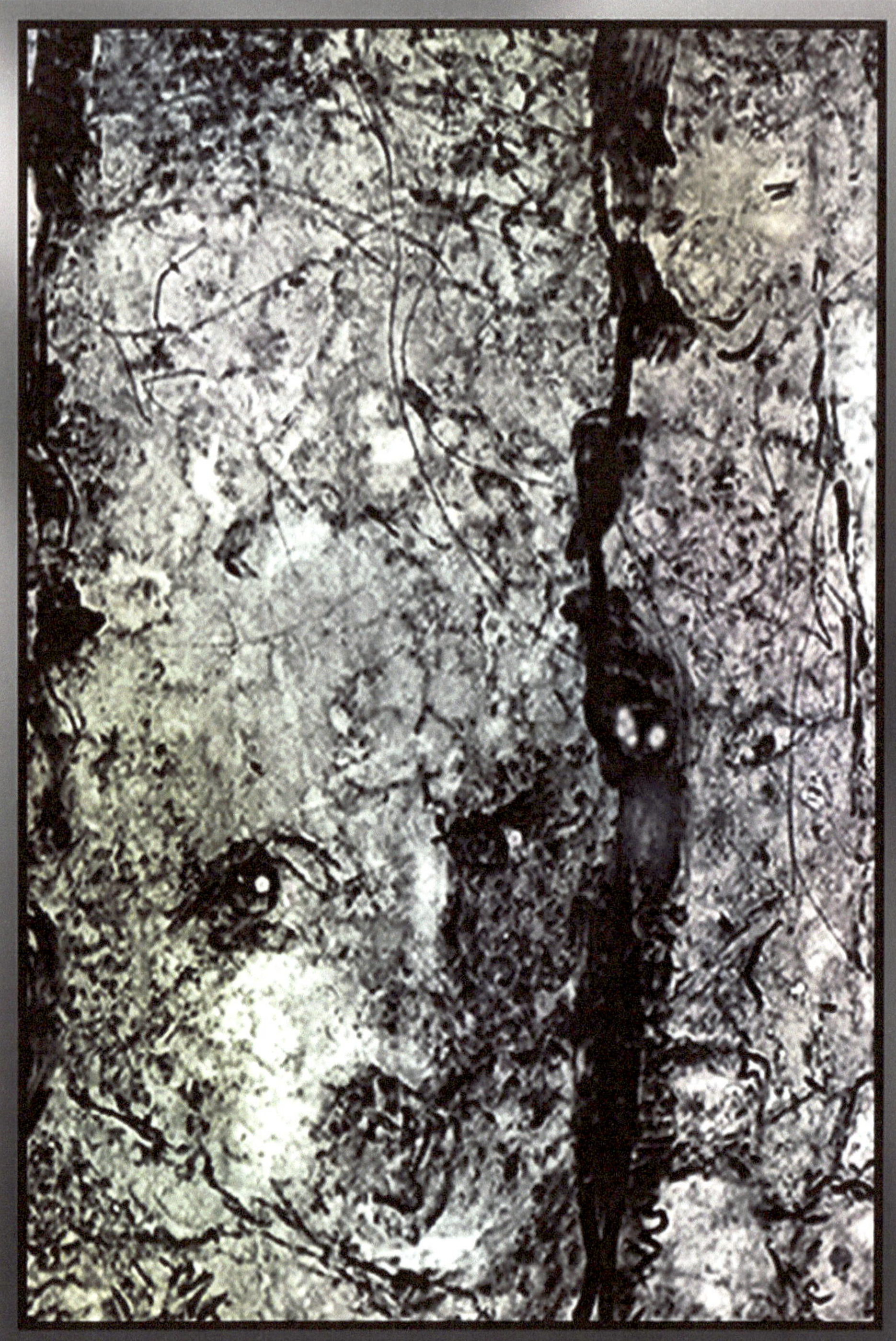

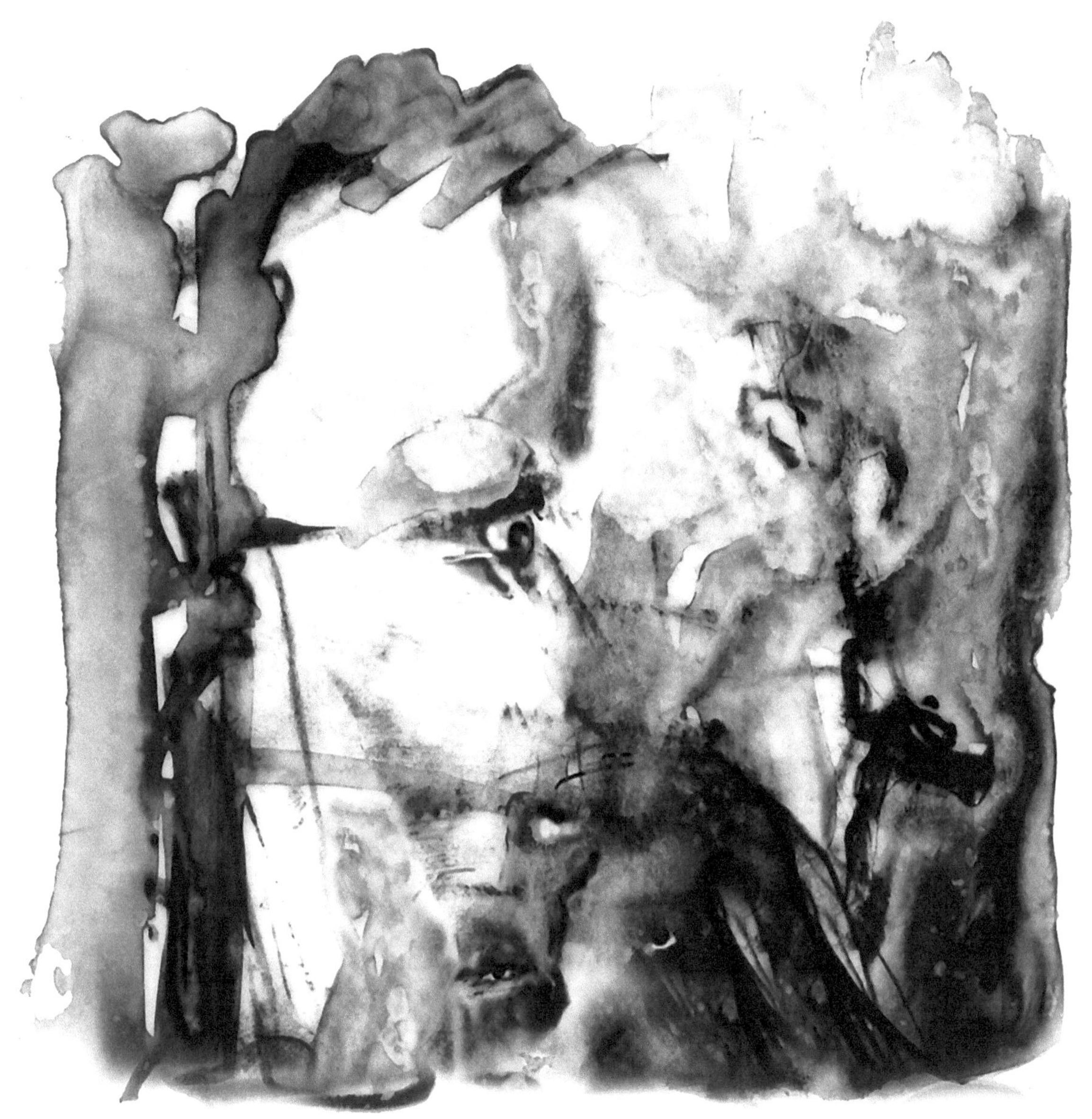

Insanity Moment

"You are the creator of everything in your life,
Nothing happens that you have not called to you."
~Pat Rodergast, Emmanuel's Book,1985

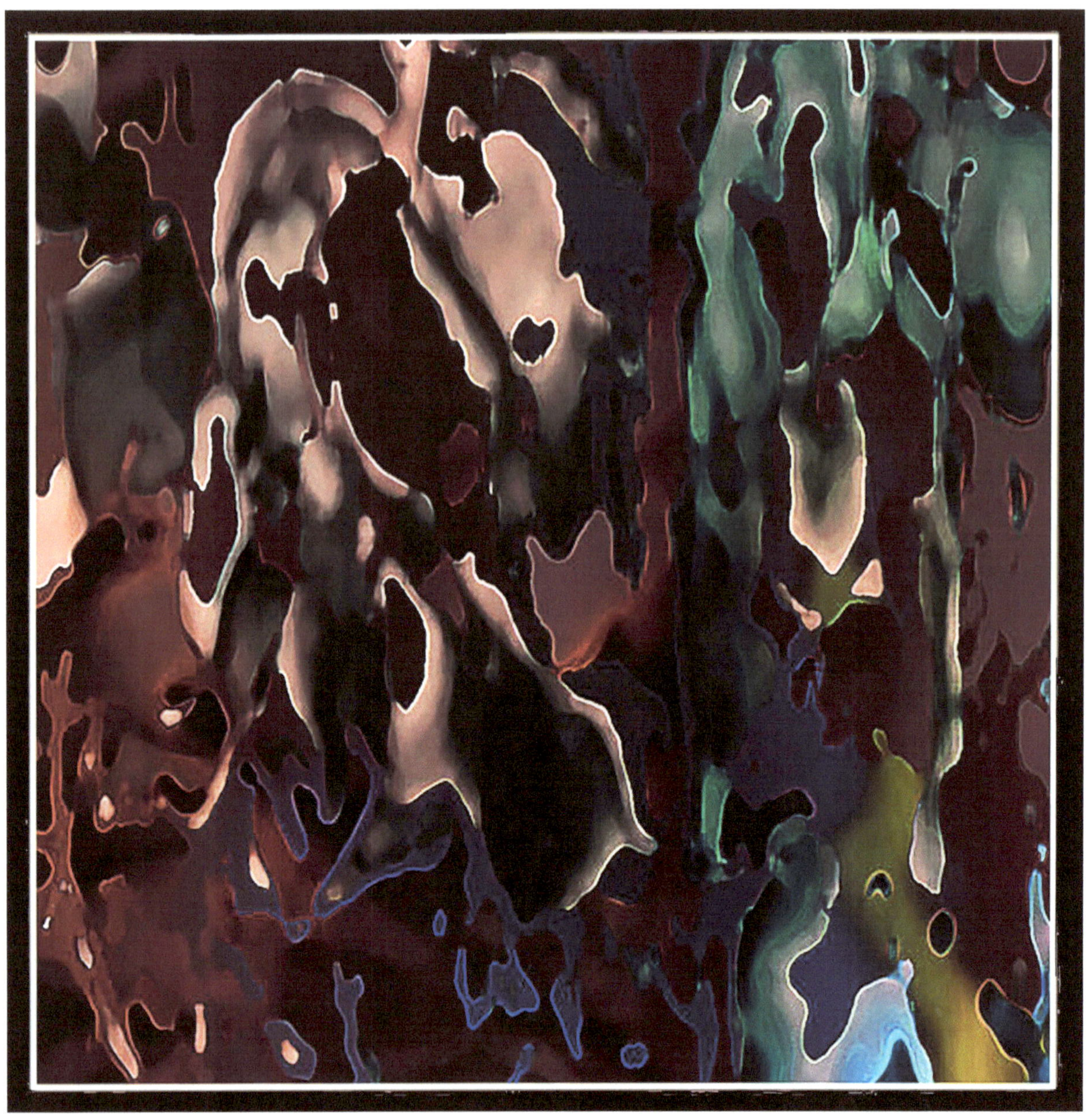

The Whole Rainbow

"The universe is not an intellectual exercise; we cannot understand it, we must look at the whole rainbow, not just one color."

~Mellen-Thomas, Messages from the Light

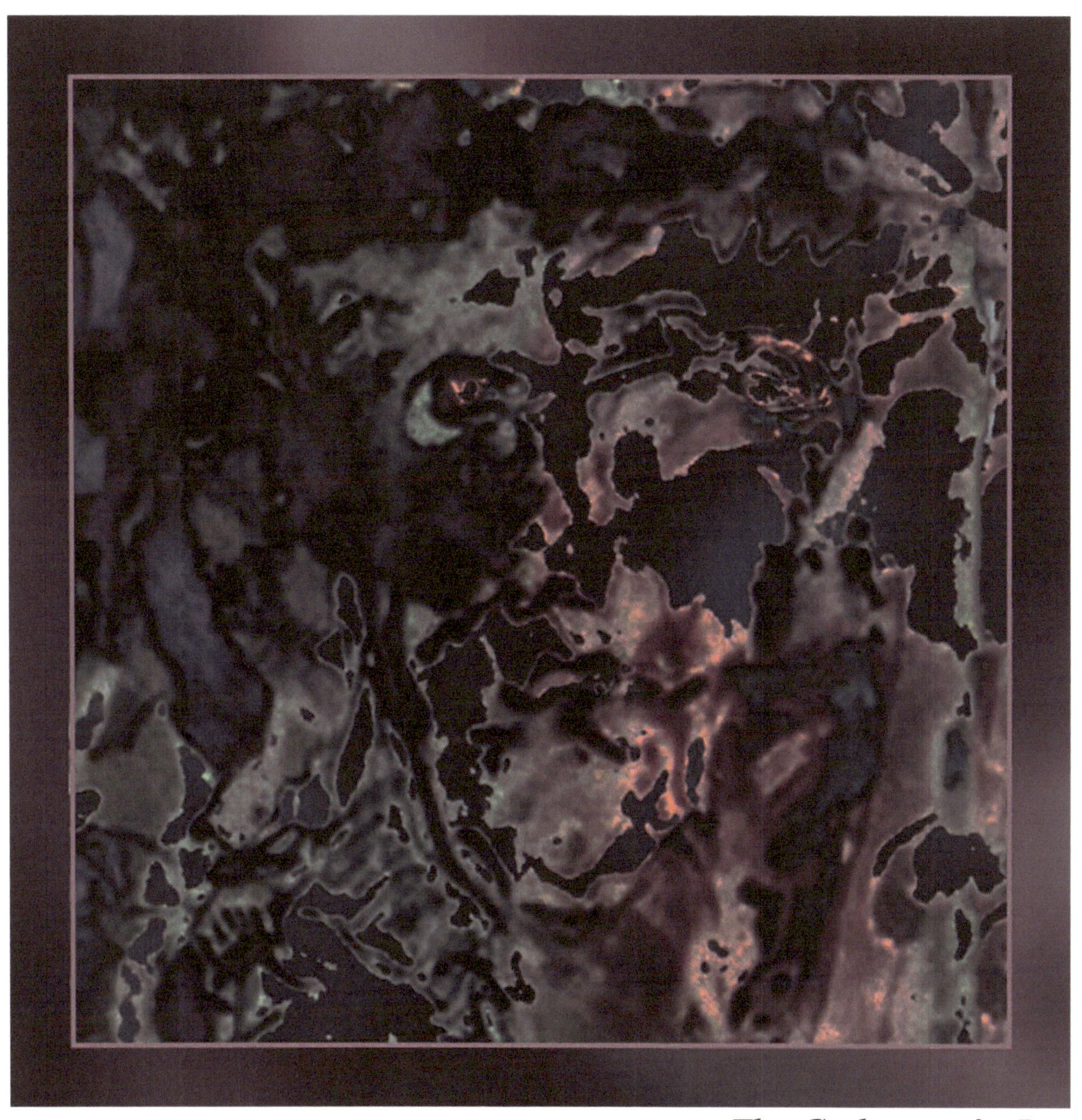

The Gathering,3e Detail 1

"Some science fiction luminaries such as Jules Verne and Gene Roddenberry were more accurate in their visions of the future than any psychics or prophets."

~Mellen Thomas, Messages from the Light

The Jules Verne Effect

Jules Verne wrote about things that did not exist,
technology that did not exist in his time.
And all the children that read those books went out
and invented those things and more.
Everything you see on Star Trek (Gene Roddenberry)
will be manifested. The children who watch these things
will make all of them, including replication technology,
teleportation, healing with light and more.

~Mellen Thomas Benedict, Messages from the Light
Website: mellen-thomas.com

The Jules Verne Effect

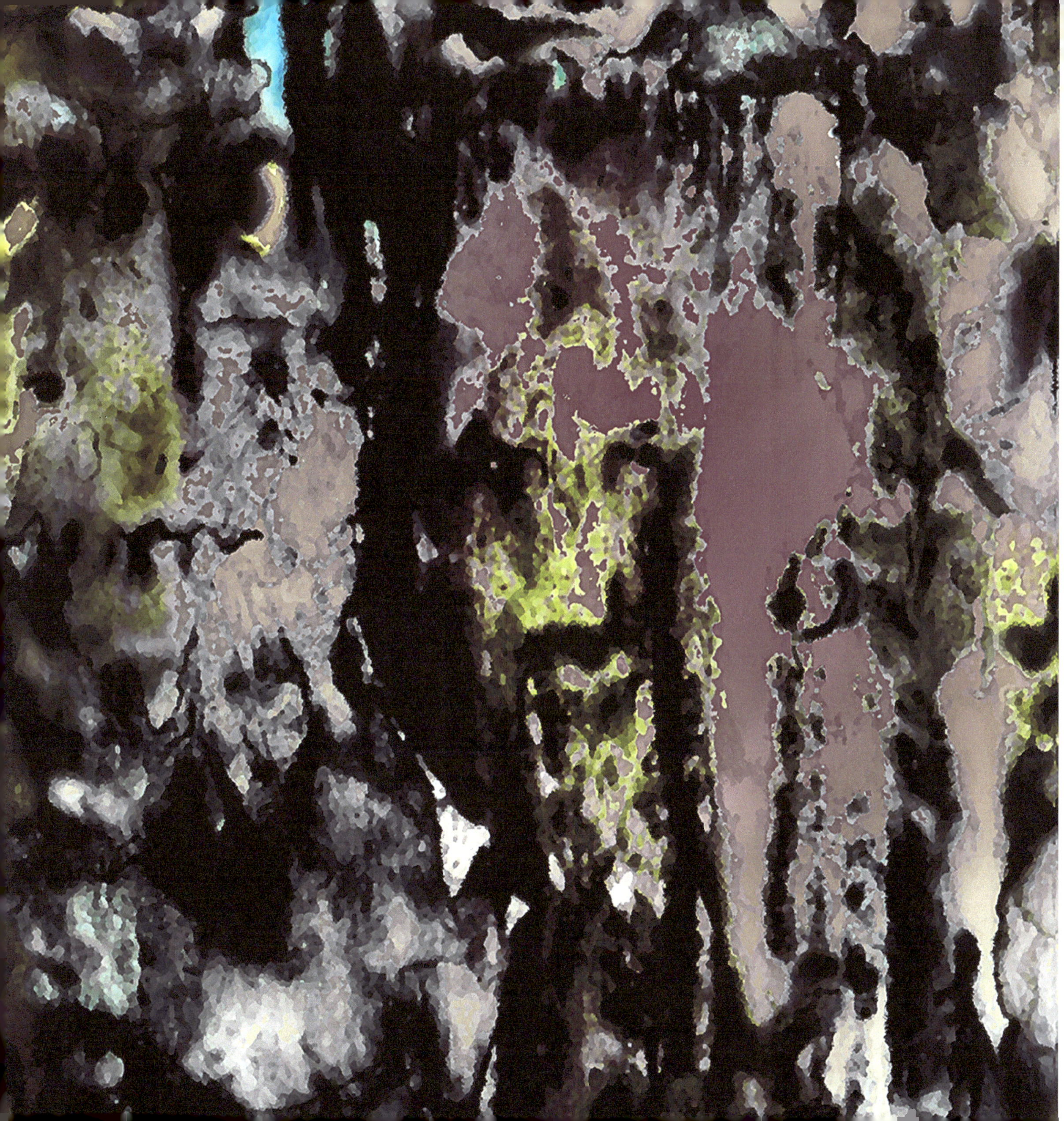

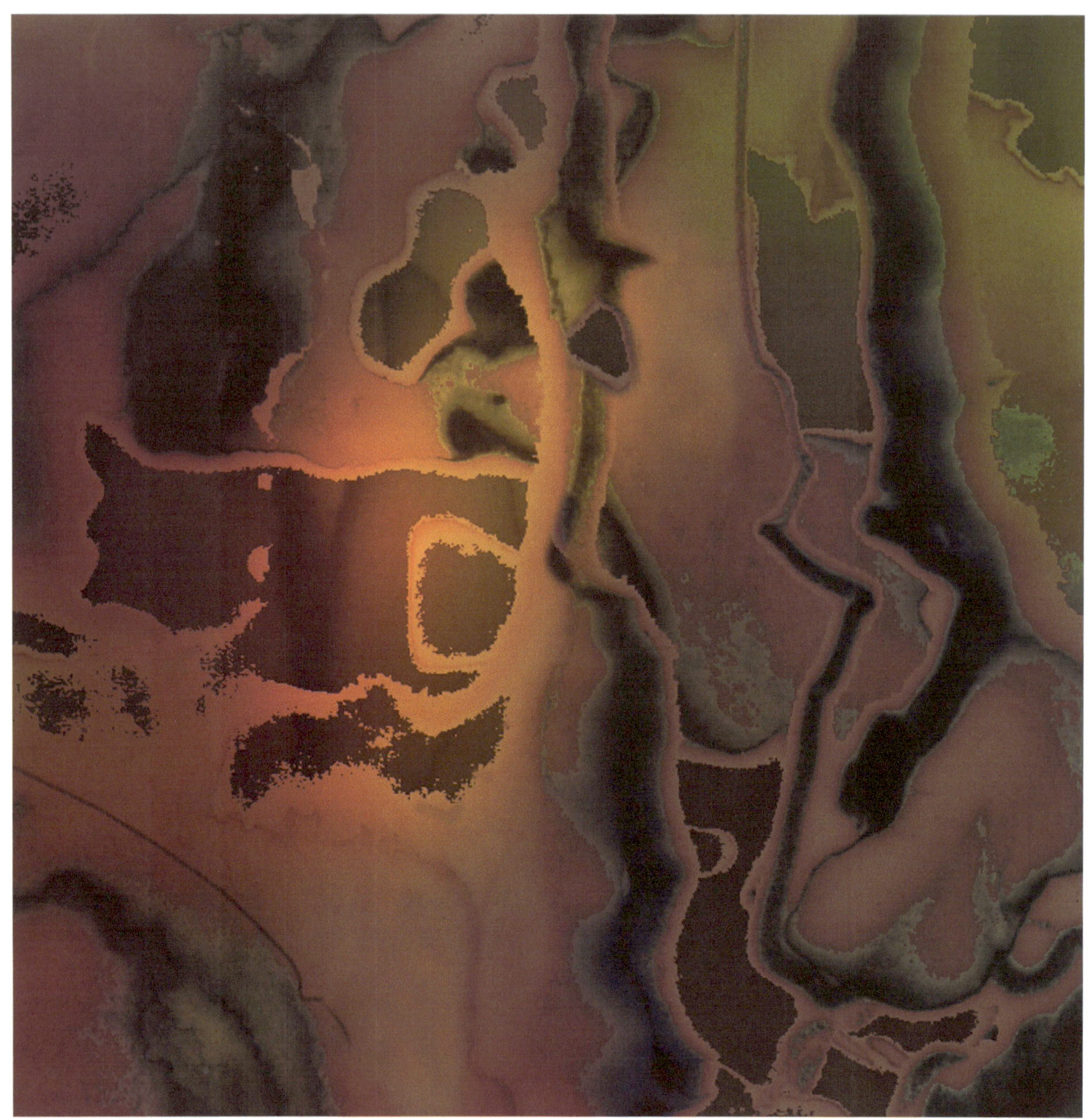

The Dream Scream

"I asked the Light,
'Why do we grow old and die?"
~Mellen-Thomas, Messages from the Light

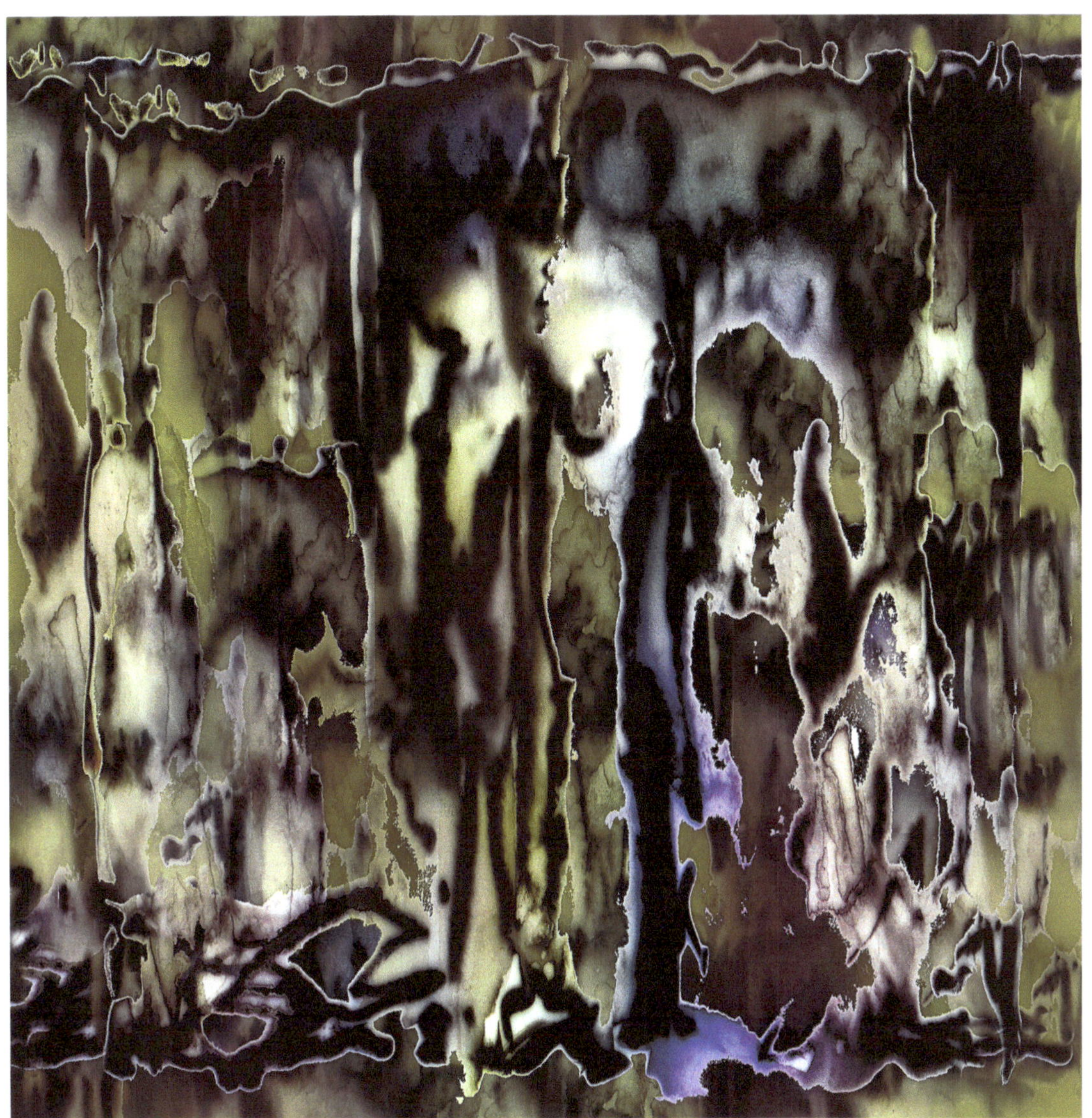

Edge of Darkness

"The future is not altered by consciousness. Rather, all possible futures really happen! Instead of a single universe proceeding in a haphazard, consciousness-altering drunkard's walk there are an infinite number of 'parallel universes,' all proceeding on well-ordered qwiffian flows into the future. And we are on all of those universe layers!" *~HUGH EVERETT III, Princeton University,1957*

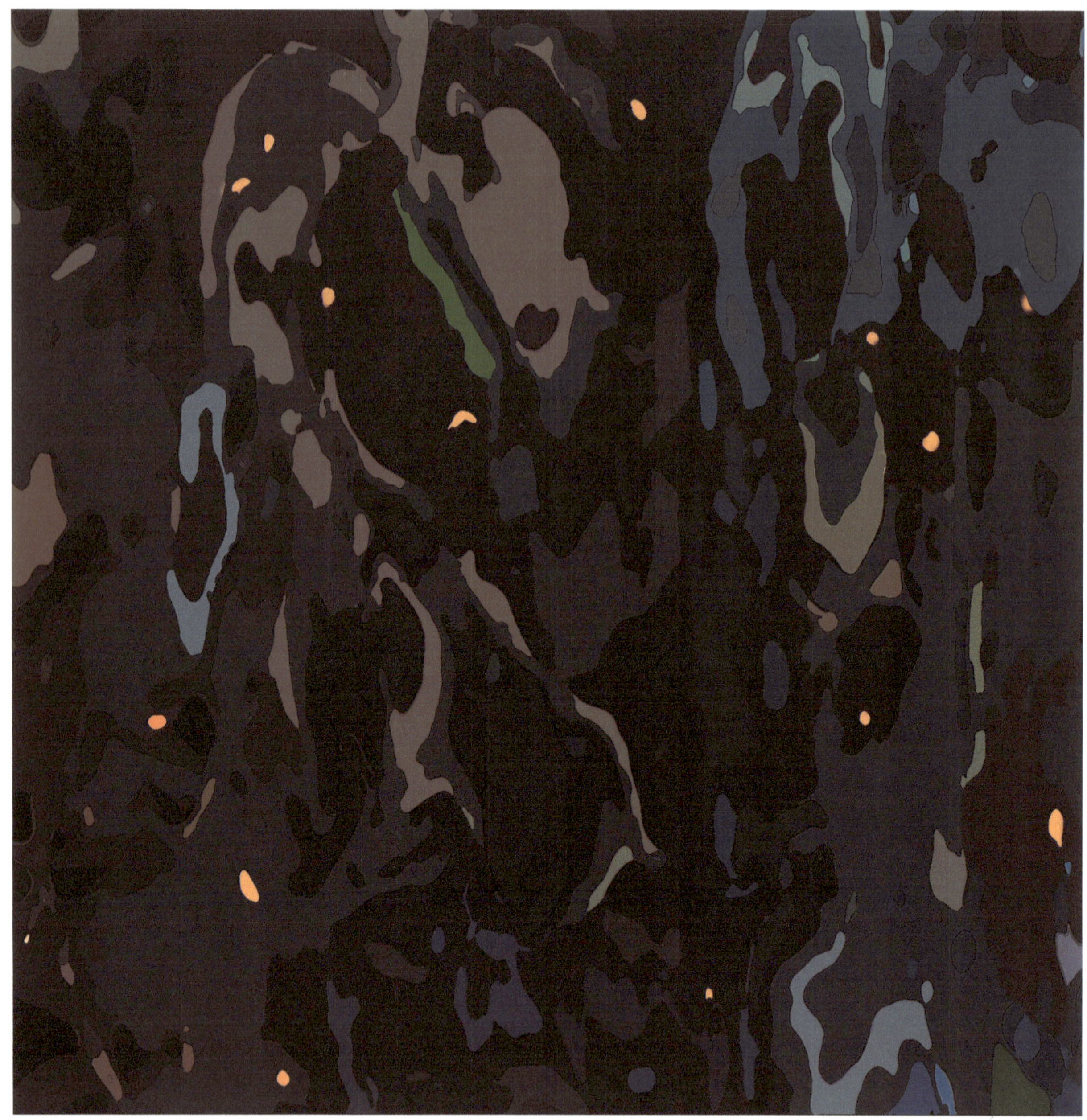

Free Spirit

"Free energy is a metaphor for
free spirit. Are we ready to be free?"
~Mellen-Thomas, Messages from the Light

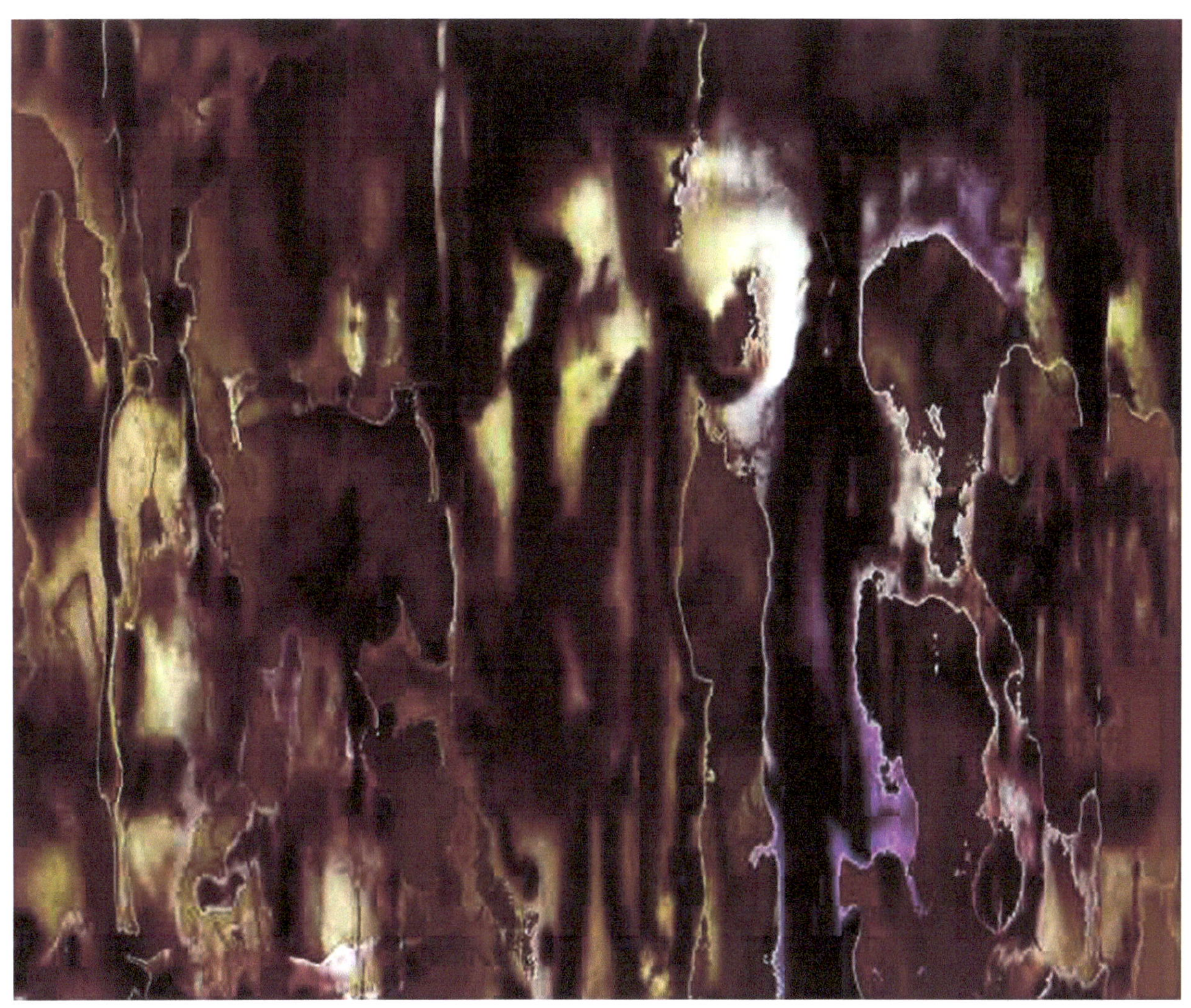

Fragmentation

"...our current way of fragmenting the world into parts not only doesn't work, but may even lead to our extinction."
~DAVID BOHM,Quantum Physicist.
MICHAEL TALBOT, The Holographic Universe, 1991

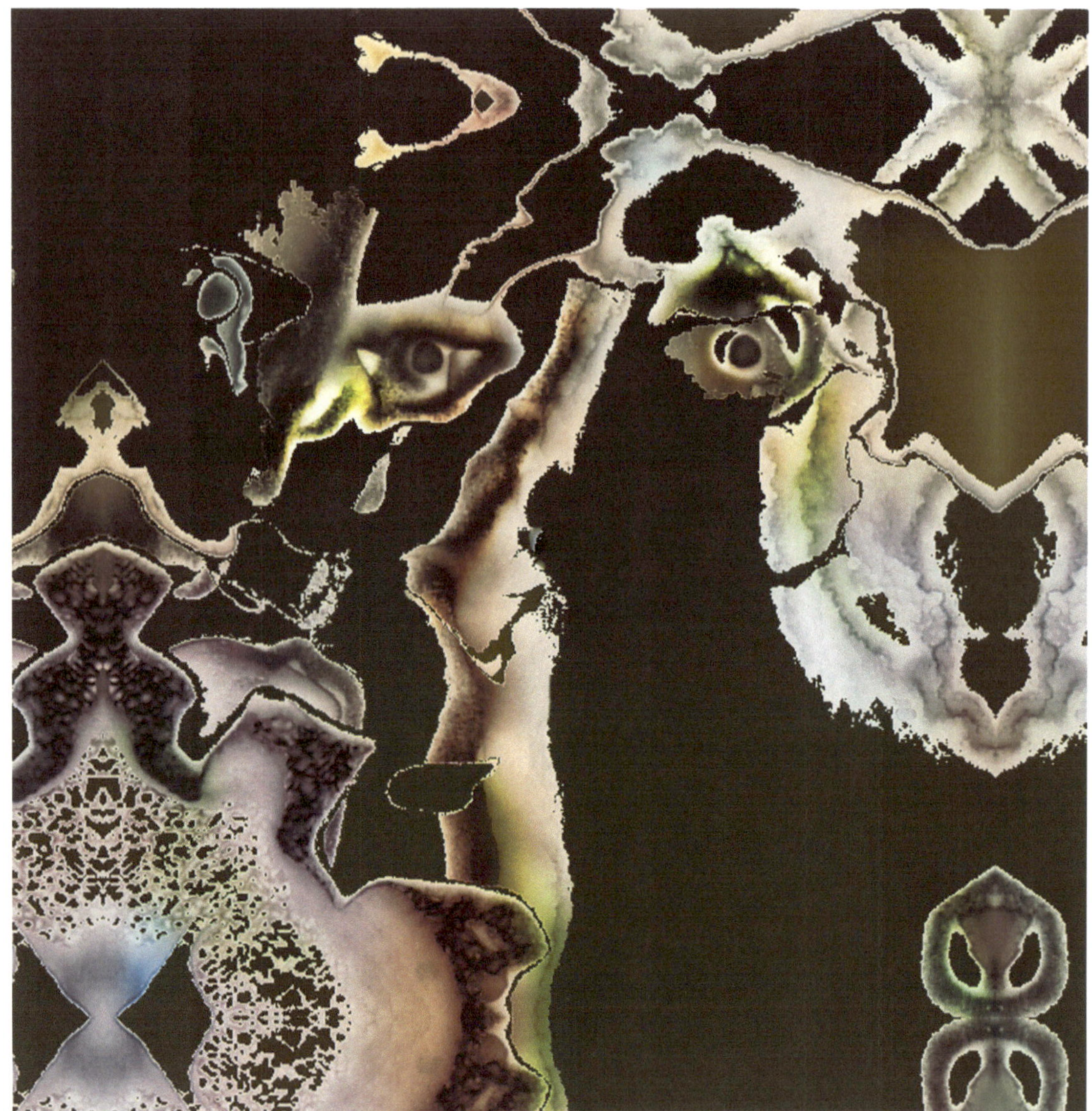

The See-Being

(CARL) "Jung concluded that myths, dreams, hallucinations, and religious visions all spring from the same source, a collective unconscious that is shared by all people."
~MICHAEL TALBOT, The Holographic Universe,1991

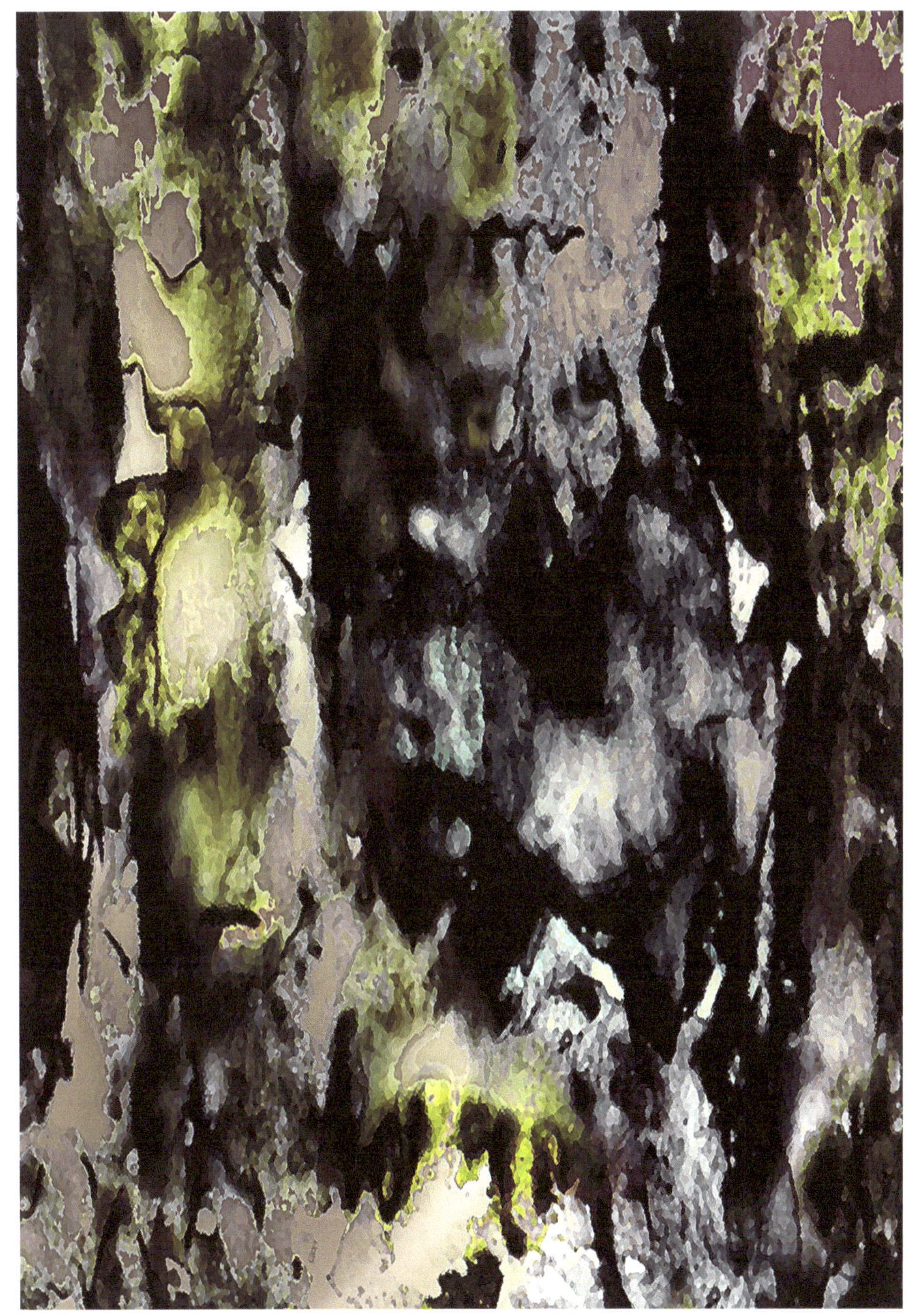

Forest Crones 3a, Detail 3

"A body without spirit is
a waste land.
A Spirit without a body is
a waste land.
With body and spirit you
can have it all."
~Mellen-Thomas,
Messages from the Light

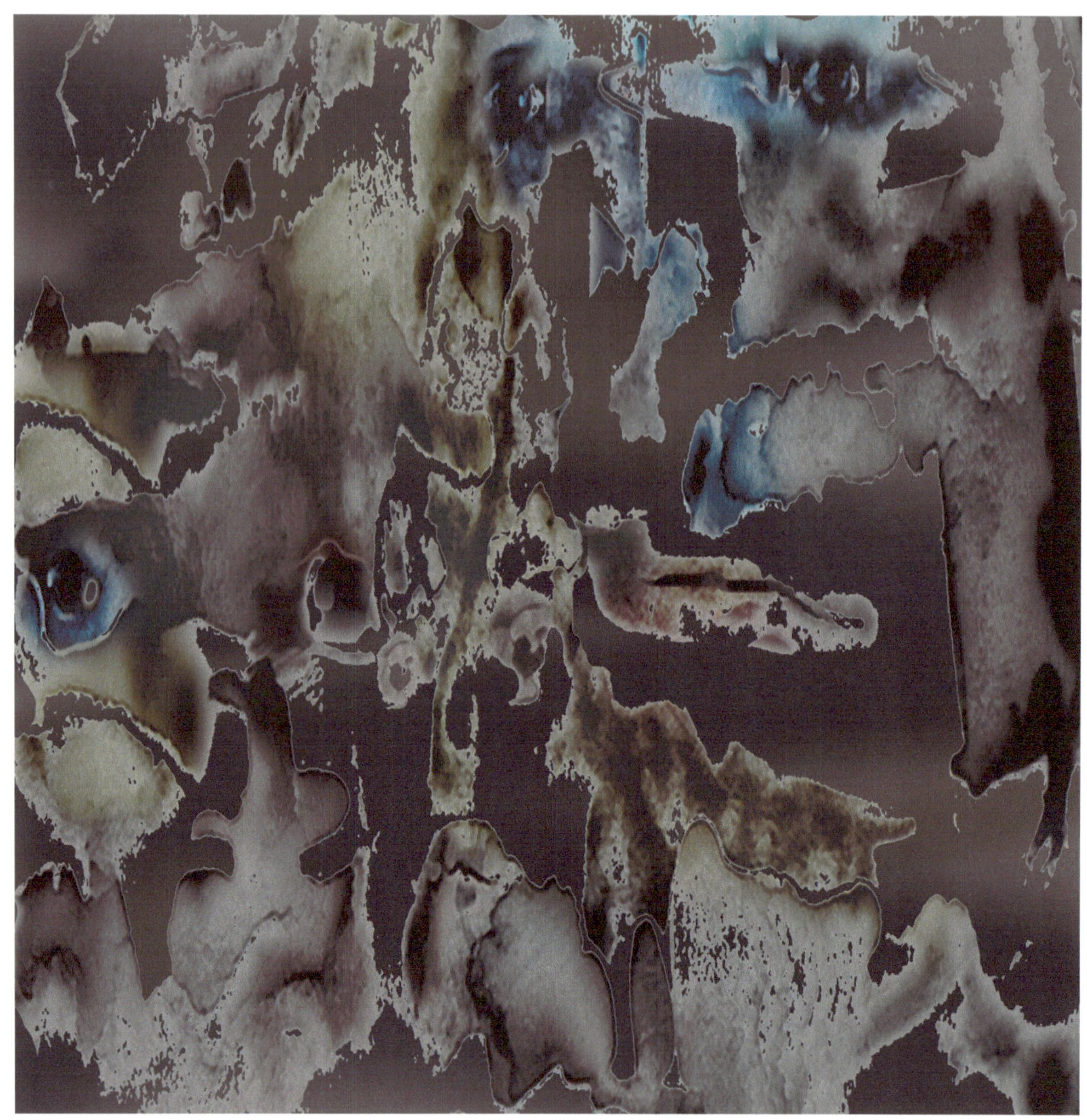

Orient Kings

"Because I could not stop for death,
He kindly stopped for me; the carriage
held but just ourselves and immortality."
~EMILY DICKINSON

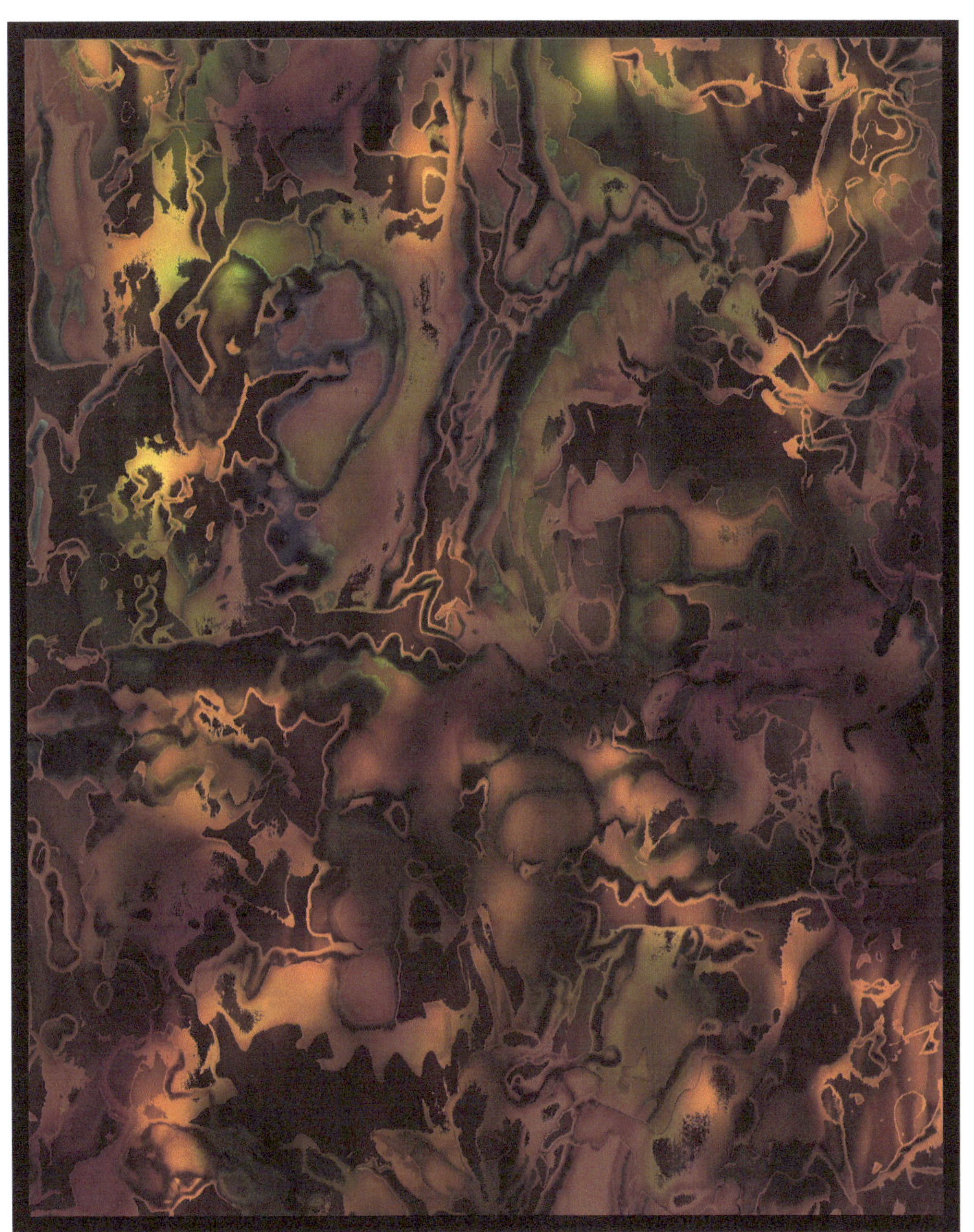

Life Is Difficult

"Accepting
'life is difficult'
...it then becomes
no longer difficult."
~ECKHART TOLLE,
The Power of Now,2001

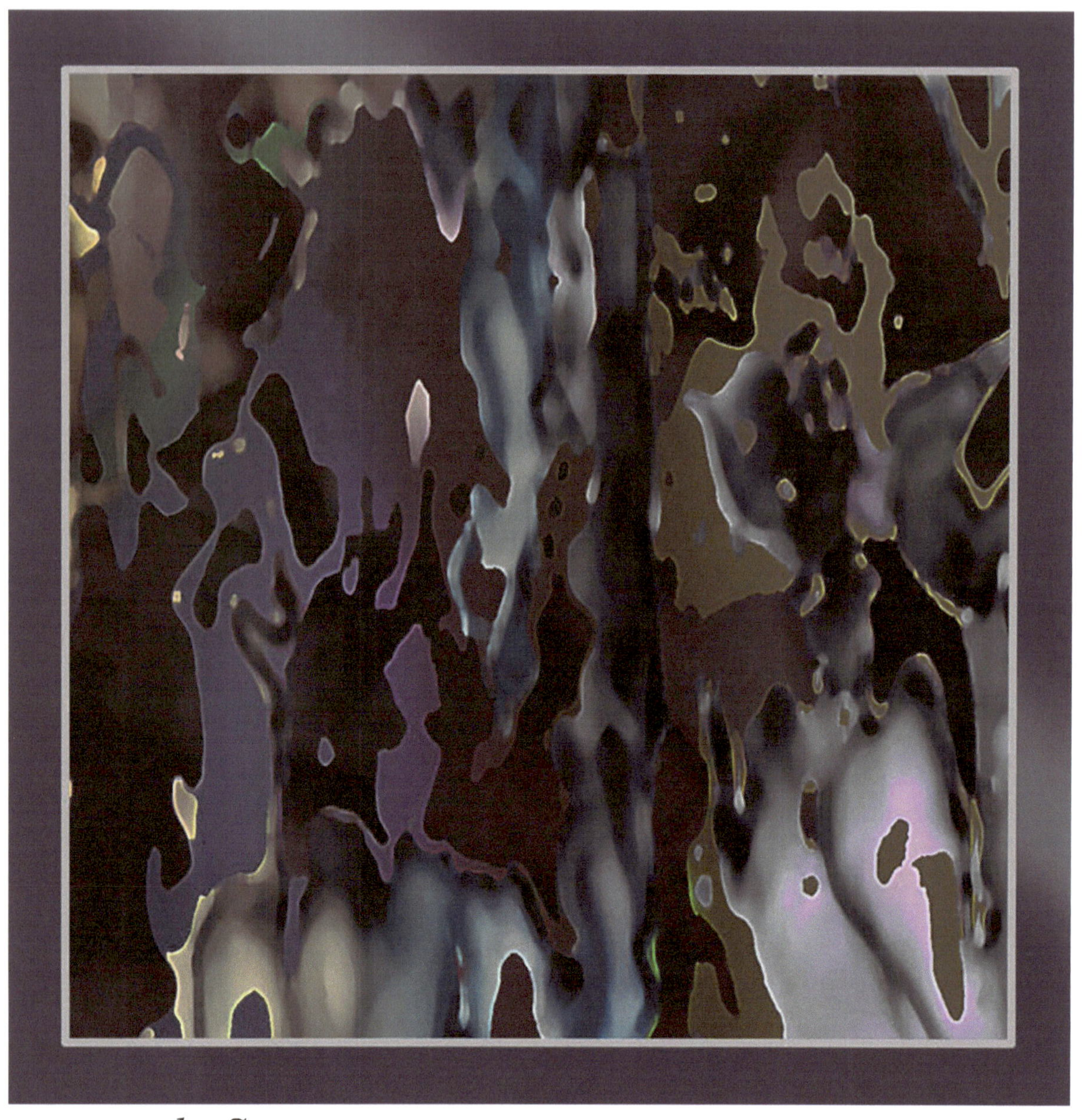

Journey to the Stars

"Our manifest destiny is to take life with us
into the stars...as where we came from originally."
~Mellen-Thomas, Messages from the Light

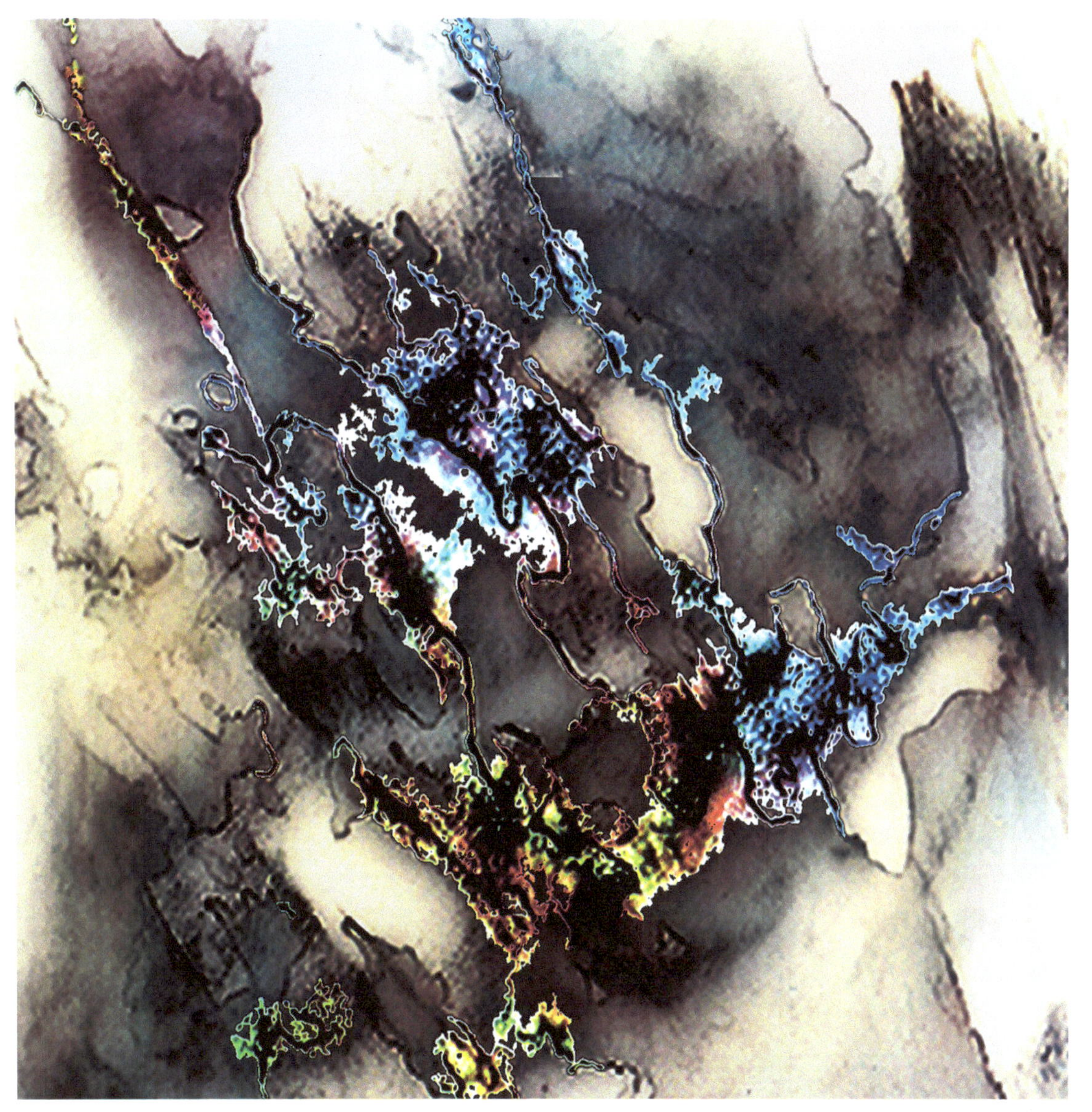

Synaptic Delight

"When your passion awakens, your soul becomes young and free and dances again...true vitality is hidden within longing."
*~JOHN O'DONOHUE,Anam Cara, a Book of Celtic Wisdom,*1997

Tip of Evolution

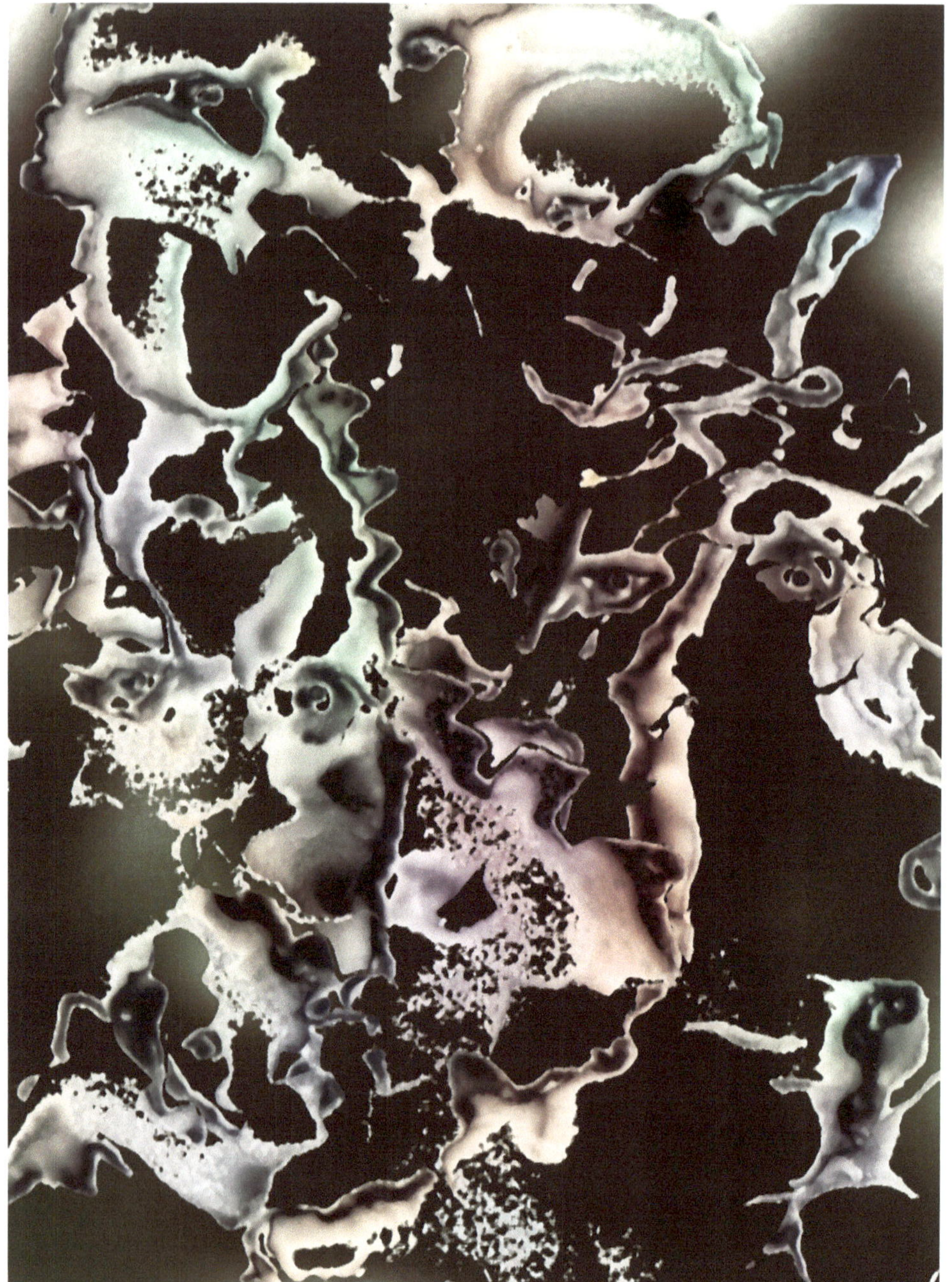

"Creation has just begun;
the future is so bright.
We've all ready made it.
Our survival...
it's inevitable."
~Mellen-Thomas,
Messages from the Light

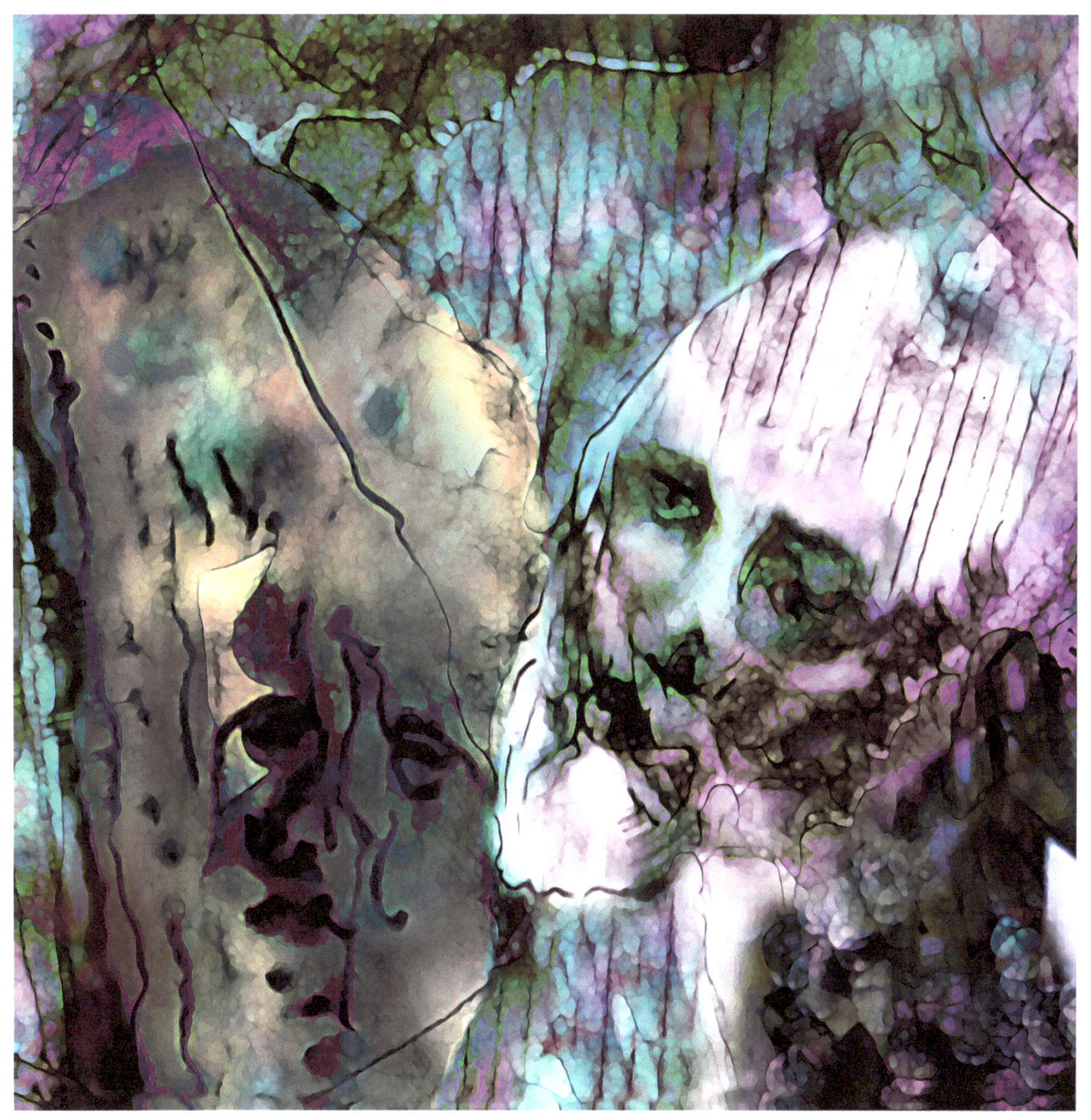

Mangled Togetherness, Blend2 Detail

You might ask: What is the purpose of your life?
"Chop wood, carry water
...then the mundane becomes sacred,
...earth becomes heaven."

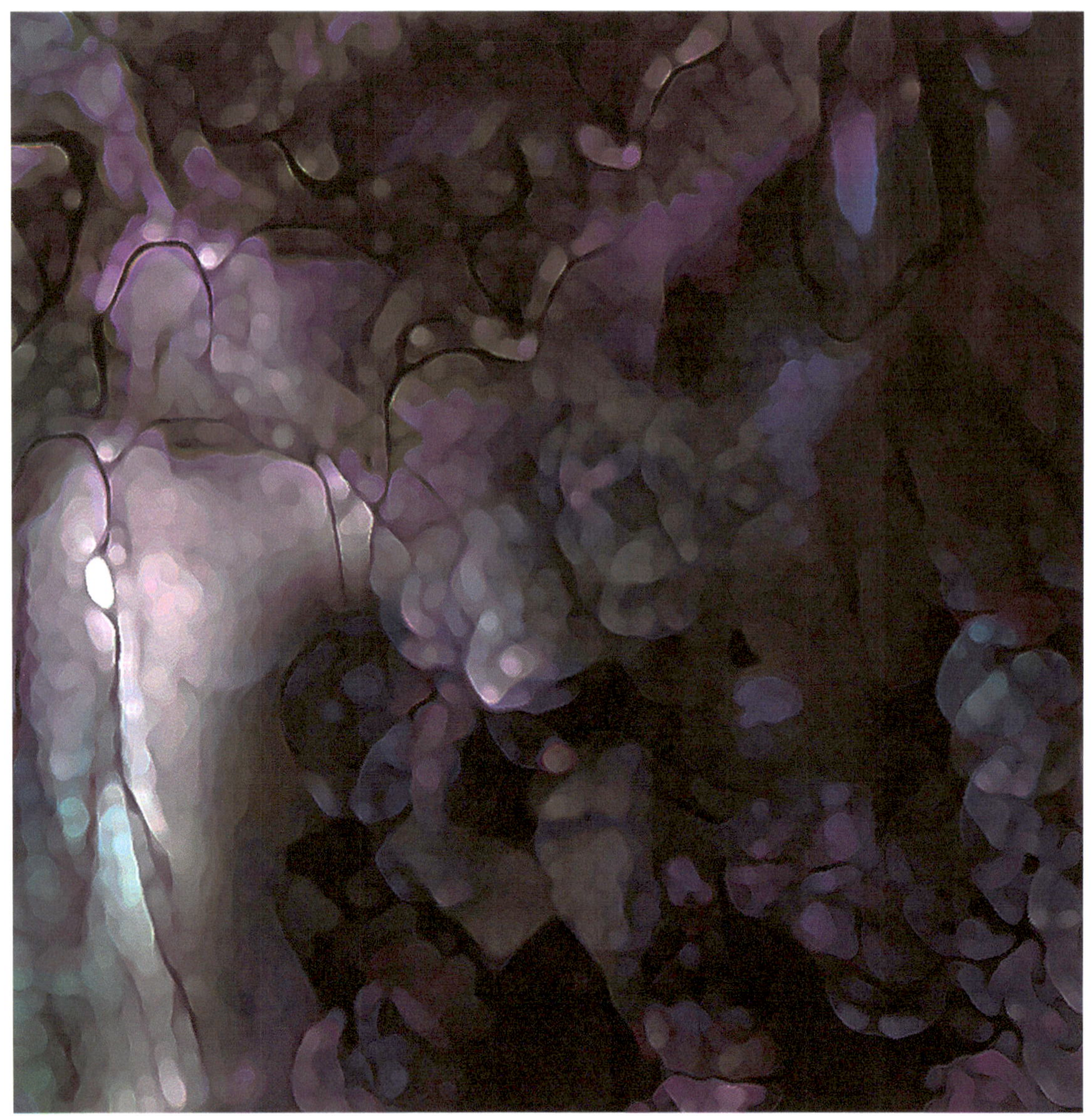

Out Beyond Ideas

"Out beyond ideas of
Wrong doing and Right doing…
There is a Field.
I'll meet you there." ~Rumi

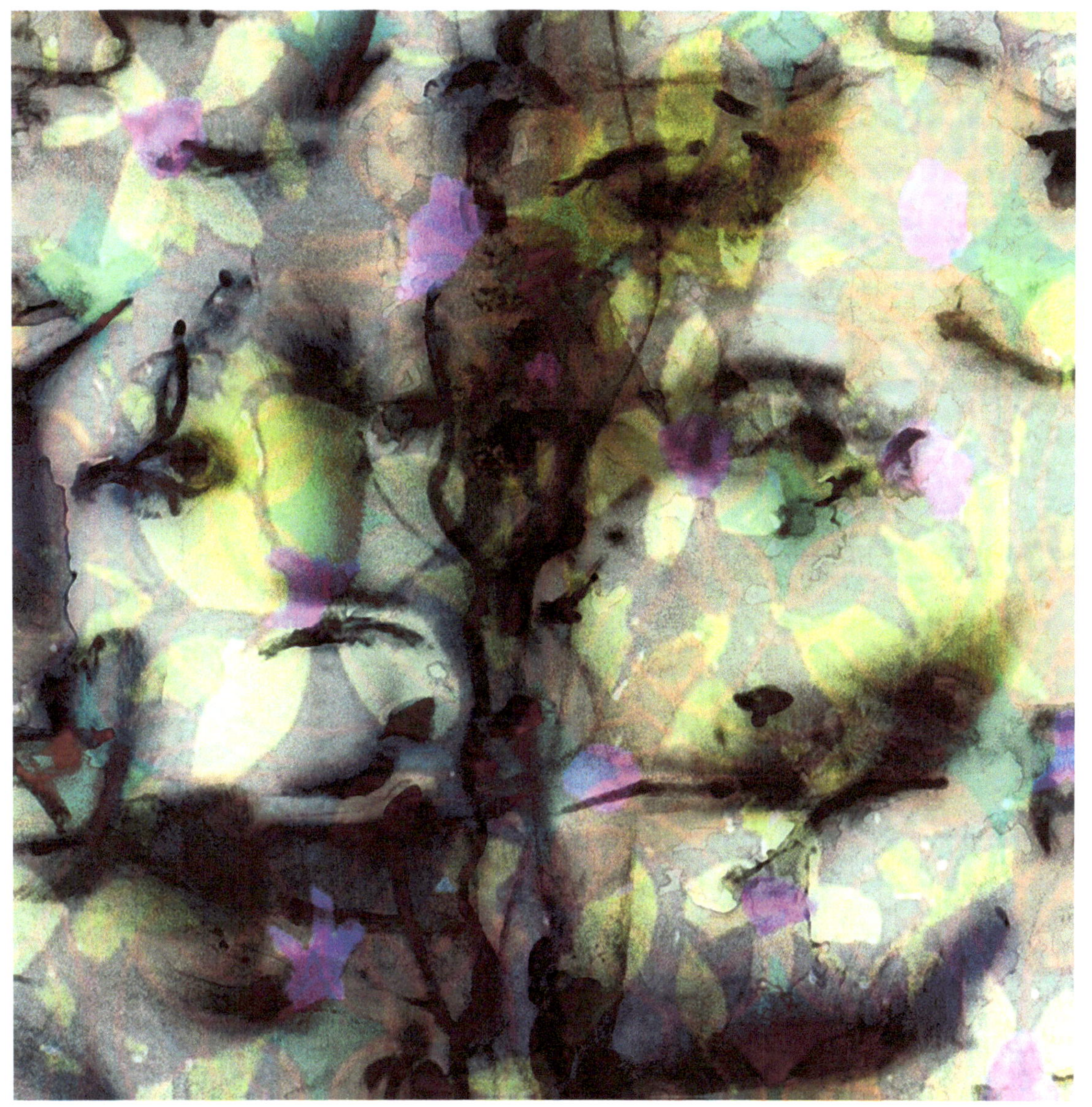

My Way

"The time has come, the walrus said to talk of many things:
Of shoes and ships and sealing wax, of cabbages and kings.
And why the sea is boiling hot and whether pigs have wings."
~LEWIS CARROLE

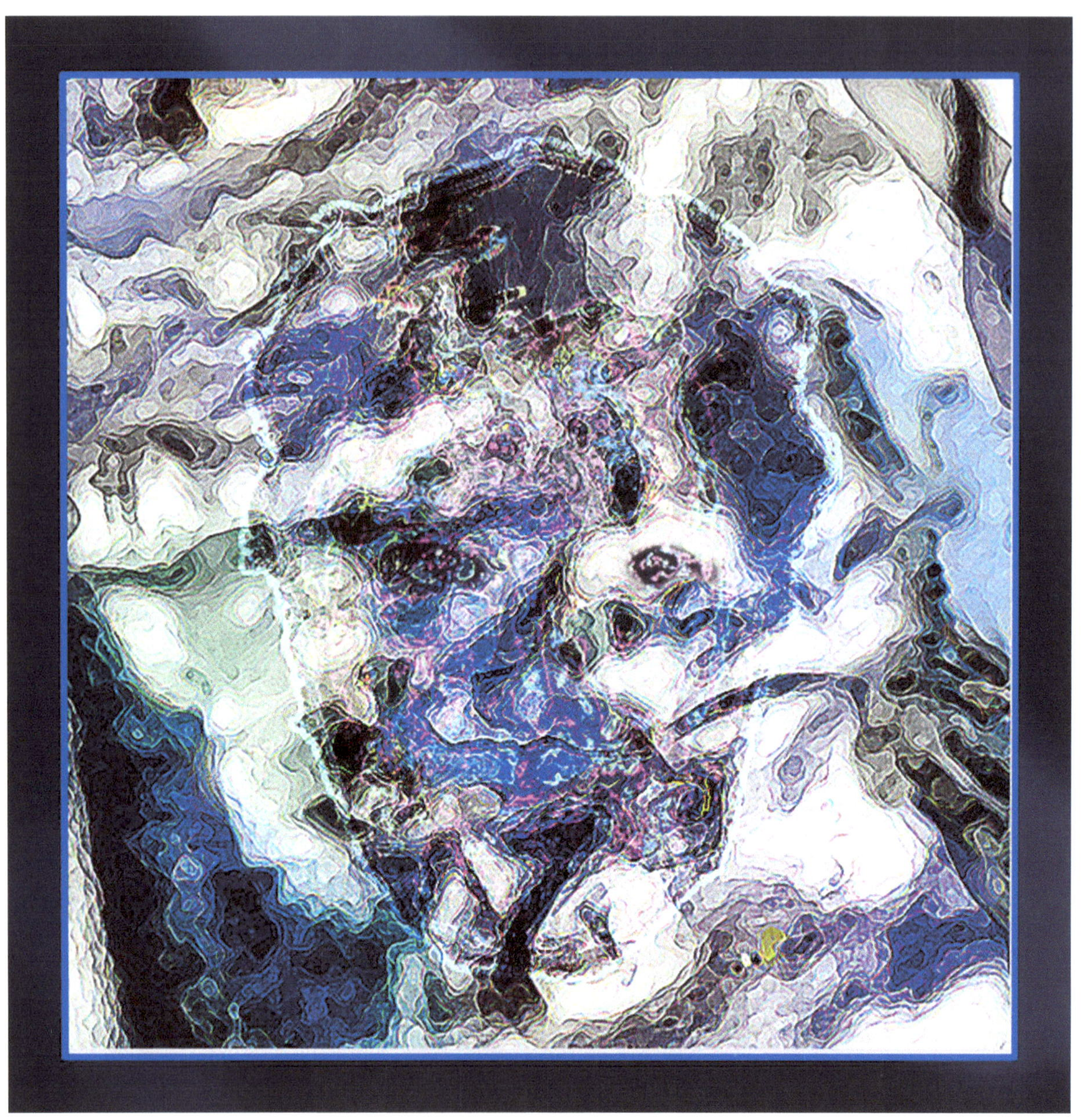

Who Are You?

"I'm nobody, who are you?"
~EMILY DICKINSON

A Brief Bio

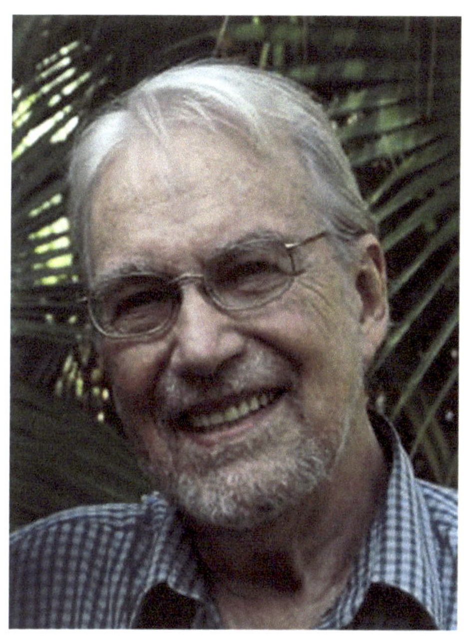

Since the early 1950's I have been continually involved with visual arts: BA degree from Pennsylvania State University, fine arts major; MA degree from Columbia University, Teachers' College, fine arts major; Parsons School of Design, advertising curriculum; Brooklyn Museum of Art, oil painting with Reuben Tam; extensive professonal experience in textile design, packaging design graphics, corporate identitiy programs, and finally teaching 22 years at the Fashion Institute of Technology (State University of New York) in New York City.

At FIT I taught textile (graphic) design from January 1975 to October 1997 in the Textile/Surface Design Department. Classes covered products from Home Furnishings to Apparel Fabric Prints; color fundamentals for beginning students; writing syllabi for advanced design classes in the upper division curriculum. The focus was on the current marketplace needs as well as the print technology necessary for industry. While at FIT, in collaboration with a fellow faculty member, Dorothy Wolfthal, we wrote the department textbook: *Textile Print Design*, Fairchild Publications, 1987.

Upon retiring from teaching I have developed my own unique approach to art and the creative processes. At the core of this work are drawing meditations. Inspired by Carl Jung, (the psychology of the mind), Anton Erhnesweig (the education of vision), Leonardo da Vinci (on creativity), and by artists such as Hieronymous Bosch, William Blake, Odilon Redon, Max Ernst & Giorgio Morandi to name a few, I continue to 'draw forth' MINDWORKS images from the unconscious mind.

Richard Fisher

www.ingramcontent.com/pod-product-compliance
Lightning Source LLC
LaVergne TN
LVHW070145110826
845147LV00002B/331